Dharma

(Volume 1)

Dharma

(Volume 1)

by
Vajra Master Samantha Chou

Translated by
Janny Chow

Purple Lotus Temple
San Bruno, California, USA.

Dharma

(Volume 1)

First Edition

Copyright © 2008 by Purple Lotus Temple, San Bruno, California

ISBN 1-881493-11-3

Printed in Hong Kong

Acknowledgments

The translator would like to thank the following persons for making this book possible:

Living Buddha Lian-sheng Sheng-yen Lu for His blessing and guidance; Vajra Master Samantha Chou for her inspiring talks and encouragement and support; Emmy Yu for transcribing the tapes into Chinese texts; Pamela Ziv Johnson and Christine Chan for editing; Lama Lian-wa for desktop publishing; and Lama Lian-yang (Alfred Wang) for the cover design.

Janny Chow

A Note from the Translator

Vajra Master Samantha Chou, the resident master at Purple Lotus Temple, a local chapter of the True Buddha School in the San Francisco Bay Area and the founder of the Purple Lotus Buddhist School of Union City, California, is a realized Buddhist master of great wisdom and compassion.

This book consists of nine selected dharma discourses delivered by Master Samantha over a span of eight years, from 1990 through 1998. Most of the articles have appeared previously in the *Purple Lotus Journal*. Master Samantha is noted for her indefatigable energy, leading weekly impromptu discourses as well as traveling internationally for numerous special ceremonies and lectures. So, indeed these nine discourses represent only a small sampling of her treasury of talks.

I have known Master Samantha since 1987 and have attended group meditations and practiced the True Buddha Tantric Dharma at the Purple Lotus Temple all this time. All these years, I am moved, by every talk, with the desire to translate and share every teaching with all beings.

Master Samantha has never been one to prepare for her talks due to her demanding schedule serving multiple roles as Buddhist master, counselor, wife, mother, and miracle worker. Yet, from the moment she sits upon the teaching chair, she launches into engaging, in depth, discourses full of humor and wisdom, opening our contracted hearts in the process.

After listening to Master's discourses, one might say that her experiences are truly extraordinary. Her exceptional ability to communicate with the psychic world has proved to be an inexhaustible resource of captivating subject matter for her audiences. Yet Master Samantha's realization is grounded in a level deeper than that of the body-mind, psychic, and subtle realms. Her stories about karma, attached spirits, and human relationships come from a heart of genuine compassion and unconditional love that embraces and includes all beings. Even if only for a moment, exposure to messages in her talks invokes a listener's heart to respond and expand.

I hope readers will find these talks educational and enlightening. May people who have affinity with the True Buddha Tantric Dharma be inspired and generate enough interest to take refuge in our Root Guru, Living Buddha Lian-sheng Sheng-yen Lu and to take up the transformational practice of the True Buddha Tantric Dharma.

Janny Chow
July 2007

Table of Contents

Acknowledgments v

A Note from the Translator vi

Introduction – The Purple Lotus 1

   1.   On the Dharma Trip to Southeast Asia 22

   2.   On Reincarnation and Cultivation 47

   3.   Bodhicitta 56

   4.   Reflections on "Birthdays" 64

   5.   Kuan Yin Ceremony in Houston 69

   6.   A Word from Master in 1995 114

   7.   Karma and Destiny 118

   8.   Key to Enlightenment 132

   9.   Present Life Karma....................................151

Appendix 163

   Impressions of Master Samantha 165

His Holiness Living Buddha Lian-sheng and Master
Samantha in Vancouver, September 19, 2006.

Living Buddha Lian-sheng with Master Samantha and Lamas
at Purple Lotus Buddhist School, March 30, 2007.

Appearance of Mantra Wheel Light during Blessing Ceremony by Master in Indonesia in Dec 2006.

Purification light on 09/11/2002 (in PLBS, Union City, Ca) during a memorial service for the people perished in 911 a year ago.

Master was about to put on the Five Buddhas Crown before a ceremony in Malaysia in April, 1994.

Master conducting a Bardo Deliverance Ceremony for the deceased and donating food and money to the survivors of the 2004 Tsunami (Feb 2005, Indonesia).

Introduction:

The Purple Lotus
Vajra Master Samantha Chou

The First Spiritual Experiences

Vajra Master Samantha Chou was born and grew up in Taiwan. She is a graduate of a Protestant college in Taipei. In her earlier years, she looked to Christianity to find answers to her problems and life's questions. However, she was unable to find practices that could satisfy her curiosity and interest.

After her marriage to Andrew Chou, Samantha emigrated from Taiwan to Canada, and resided in Vancouver, British Columbia for ten and a half years. Then, in July 1984, she had a number of dreams which marked the beginning of an incredible series of events. For seven consecutive nights, she dreamt of many Buddhas and Bodhisattvas which she did not recognize. On the final day, acting on an inexplicable impulse, she made a long distance telephone call to her mother in Taiwan, unaware of the lateness of the hour in Taipei.

At about the same time, her mother, Mrs Wang, was in the middle of a dream. In her dream, Mrs. Wang was inside a temple and all the worshippers were handing her incense sticks. She then heard someone call her name, so she handed the bundle of incense sticks that had accumulated in her hands over to her daughter, Samantha. It was at this point that she was awakened by the phone call from Vancouver. While still under the influence of the dream state, Mrs. Wang asked Samantha to fly back to Taipei to visit her.

Thus, Samantha booked a flight back to Taiwan. While on the airplane, she read a Chinese magazine a friend had given her just prior to departure and came upon an article written by the famous Chinese writer, San Mou. In that article, San Mou gave an account of how she had tried to make contact with her deceased husband through a medium in Taipei by the name of Mr. Lue. This piqued Samantha's curiosity and she decided to seek out the medium upon arrival to attempt to contact her father and grandmother who had passed away when Samantha was a child. Little did she know, the encounter would lead to dramatic life changes, transforming her from an ordinary housewife to a Buddhist Master devoted to the propagation of Buddhism.

Samantha met with Mr. Lue in August of 1984. Mr. Lue's channeling method, which he had learned from his father, was quite unusual. His method allowed the participants to see and sense for themselves the spiritual realm. In her first session, Samantha was blindfolded and seated while Mr. Lue performed some rituals and recited incantations. Samantha's body began swaying in circles. She entered a trance-like state, and a deity came and led her to see both her grandmother and her father, who were inhabiting two completely different realms of disembodied existence.

At the end of the session, Samantha removed her blindfold to find, unexpectedly, many spectators in the room. In fact, the whole session had been taped by the China Television Company for the local show "Ninety Minutes." (It was merely a coincidence that the reporters decided to visit Mr. Lue at that time, right in the middle of Samantha's session.) The TV crew requested that Samantha participate in one more session the following day.

During her second session, she was led not only to different heavenly realms but also to the Dragon King's Palace. She saw wonderful scenes not of this world. However, at the end of the session, after coming out of her trance and removing her blindfold, she realized that she could still see the deity that led her on her out-of-body trip. Mr. Lue tried, to no avail, to rid her of this "special sight" by sprinkling water on her and reciting more incantations. That night, in addition to the acquisition of this special sight, Samantha was awakened by a strong force. Bodhisattvas and deities began talking to her and giving her teachings. This continued almost every night thereafter. She went back to Mr. Lue to ask why these visions were occurring. He replied that she had been selected by the deities and there was nothing he could do to help her.

Voices from the Womb

After returning to Canada, Samantha relayed her psychic experience in Taipei to her husband. Her story was met with complete disbelief. While watching the taped session Samantha had brought back, he started laughing. Immediately the television set exploded, leaving only the sound track running – a divine warning against irreverence.

Upon returning from Taipei, Samantha suddenly stopped menstruating. After numerous, thorough medical exams, Samantha was told by her physicians that they could find nothing wrong with her. Although they could offer no explanation as to why she had stopped menstruating, they stated that, as long as she remained amenorrheic, she would be infertile. At the time, she had only one son, Phillip, and wanted very much to have a daughter.

She wrote to Mr. Lue about her concerns, and he reasoned that the deities did not want her to have any more children so that she could devote her life to serving sentient beings. Enraged by this reply, she refused to get up at night for her lessons. How could the Bodhisattvas force someone into doing something against one's will? Her refusal to have any further communication with the deities changed a month later when a voice told her that she would have a child in July 1986.

In September 1985, Samantha moved with her husband and son from Vancouver to San Francisco. One night in early November, while sleeping in her apartment in South San Francisco, she was awakened by a golden light coming through her bedroom door radiating throughout the room. A Buddha whom she intuitively knew to be Vairocana, the Great Sun Buddha, was suspended in mid-air. He spoke to her, "You are pregnant with a girl. Her name is Fu-nian (Maiden Who Gives Blessing). Recite the Diamond Sutra and Mantra and practice the Mudra as shown." Samantha instinctively bowed and paid homage to the Buddha.

The next morning she told Andrew about the incident. He thought her story was ridiculous and told her that her desperate craving for a daughter was causing her to hallucinate. Concerned, he suggested they adopt a daughter to calm her mind.

As it turned out, Samantha indeed became pregnant and a laboratory test ordered by her physician a month later confirmed the pregnancy.

One morning during her seventh month of pregnancy, Samantha was alone reading newspapers in her living room when she suddenly heard a dignified voice call out "Namo Amitabha" three times in the Taiwanese dialect. Startled and puzzled, she asked herself, "Who is reciting the Buddha's name?" A voice from her abdomen replied, "It is me, your daughter." She was not the only one who heard this voice. During a subsequent trip to Los Angeles, one of her high school friends also heard the voice from her womb.

Samantha would occasionally also hear another voice, that of a powerful male. This worried her and she began to wonder if the baby would turn out normally. When she related her concerns to her doctor, she was told that she was imagining things. When she approached a well known Buddhist Master in the San Francisco Bay Area about the phenomenon, she was told that she was possessed by demons.

Taking Refuge in Living Buddha Lian-sheng

At this point, Samantha became quite desperate. She wondered if there was anyone in this world who could give her guidance. It was at this time that a friend from Canada, Ms. Yao, gave her Living Buddha Lian-sheng's name and telephone number in Redmond, Washington. Ms. Yao had just taken refuge in Grand Master Lu and believed that, with the kind of unusual occurrences Samantha was experiencing, only Grand Master Lu could offer her help.

Immediately Samantha placed a telephone call to Redmond, Washington and made an appointment to meet Grand Master Lu. The appointment was set for 4:00 p.m. on the 29th of March, 1986. The entire night after making the call, Samantha dreamt of Grand Master Lu. In her dreams, the Grand Master's head was shaven, like a monk's, and they conversed with each other for a long time. On the day of the appointment, Ms. Yao met Samantha at the airport. When Samantha told her about the dream, Ms. Yao flatly denied its authenticity as Grand Master had a full head of hair. When they arrived at Ling Shen Ching Tze, the temple in Redmond, Ms. Yao found to her astonishment that Grand Master's head was indeed shaven! Ms. Yao had not known that Grand Master had taken the renunciation vow and had his head shaven just ten days earlier, on the 19th of March.

At 4:00 p.m., Samantha entered the True Buddha Tantric Quarter. Upon meeting Grand Master Lu face to face for the first time, she felt as if she had known him for a long time. Grand Master Lu looked silently at her, with a smile on his face. He walked over to the shrine, wrote the following words and showed them to her: "The mission given to you by Shakyamuni Buddha to help sentient beings begins now. There is a sign on your palm to prove this. The child in your womb is incarnating in the dual roles of Bodhisattva and Dharma Protector." Just as Samantha was wondering to herself what she was supposed to do, Grand Master Lu asked her to kneel and take refuge. Bewildered, she did as she was told.

At 8:00 p.m. that evening, there was to be a group practice at the Ling Shen Ching Tze. Samantha, having lost her way en route, arrived late and sat with her friend in the last row of the temple. Someone asked Grand Master how the relatively few masters of True Buddha School could cope with the huge waves of students taking refuge. Grand Master answered, "There are many conditions that lead to the finding of a master. Today we have found another one and she is the Purple Lotus, Miss

Wang (Samantha's maiden name) from San Francisco."
Initially, Samantha did not realize that Grand Master was
referring to her. Her friend nudged her and only then did
it dawn on her. As she stood up, her mind was filled with
suspicion. "Since I am a visitor from out of town, could
the Grand Master be using me to take everyone in?" she
wondered. After the group practice, Master Lian-huo
gave Samantha a copy of the group practice text, and
Grand Master simply told her to go home and practice
according to the text.

After returning home, Samantha read a dozen of
Grand Master's books. She practiced according to the
text. Initially, she was confused and thought she had to
practice the eight Personal Deity Yogas together in one
single session. She spent all her time, from after
breakfast until it was time to prepare dinner, carefully
visualizing each deity and reciting each mantra 108
times. When she made a mistake with the mudras,
whether intentionally or not, an invisible force pulled her
hands back to the correct gesture, as if she were being
observed and guided. Gradually, with more and more
practice, Samantha felt that the eight deities were starting
to respond to her.

Bardo Deliverance and Divination

Samantha had learned to recite the Rebirth
Mantra even before taking refuge in Grand Master Lu.
Around Qing Ming Day (a memorial day in Chinese

custom where people pay their respects to the deceased) April 4, 1985, she began reciting the Rebirth Mantra for her ancestors, as well as for acquaintances who had passed away. As she recited, she saw the mantra transform into a lotus of light with many hands reaching out to catch its light. She knew that the lotus light was guiding the deceased toward the Western Paradise of Ultimate Bliss, the Pure Land of Amitabha Buddha.

The birth of Samantha's daughter, Megia, was accompanied by many unusual signs. Megia gave her mother some very specific instructions regarding the preparations for her birth, as well as whom she would see during the first month of her life. After she was born, Megia often helped Samantha solve problems for people who were now seeking her for consultation and divination. One time Samantha became ill after intervening in someone's karmic hindrance problem. One of Samantha's arms and legs stiffened, disabling her. At the time her transcendental power had not yet fully developed. That night, after leaving Megia alone for a moment, Samantha returned to find the baby doubled over on the floor, crying inconsolably. Upset that the dharma protectors had not taken care of Megia, Samantha asked the Bodhisattvas why this was so. She received no reply. The following day, a voice told Samantha that Megia had interceded on her behalf and taken over her illness. Only then did Samantha notice her arms and legs were no longer stiff and that she was moving about normally.

Introduction: The Purple Lotus

When Megia was three months old, Samantha and Megia decided to work together to convince Andrew of the psychic happenings around him. He was still very skeptical and considered himself a scientific and rational-minded individual. First, they predicted to the minute the time he would come home on a specific day. Then they asked the Buddhas to cure his hay-fever. On both occasions Andy claimed that the results were mere coincidences. Finally, Samantha made a written pact with Andrew that, if the lipoma (a growth of fatty cells) on his back would disappear, he would have to promise to uphold and support the Buddhadharma in this lifetime as well as in his future lives. Samantha then prayed to the Buddhas while visualizing light illuminating Andrew's back. Days passed. Then one day, out of the blue, Andrew thought of the growth on his back and reached his arm around to feel for it. It was gone! He almost fell out of his chair in disbelief.

Samantha found herself looking at Megia one day and her heart filled with a strong maternal love and attachment for the baby. She thought to herself, tears streaming down her cheeks, "How can I detach from my daughter and do what Grand Master is doing now, devoting myself to help all other sentient beings?" Suddenly, a huge white lotus blossom appeared in the empty space and the voice of Grand Master spoke to her, "If you cannot detach yourself from these personal sentiments, how will you embrace the whole world?" Samantha was stunned! Grand Master Lu was, indeed, an

11

enlightened being! With a single thought of him, he appeared. What little doubt she still had in Grand Master vanished completely.

With renewed confidence and faith in her guru, Samantha opened her heart completely to the cultivation of the True Buddha Tantric Dharma. Through the transformation she witnessed in her own inner life, as well as those in other students, she came to recognize that the True Buddha Dharma as taught by Grand Master is, indeed, a valid and effective method to lead one back to one's Buddha Nature. By sincerely devoting herself to the three keys to cultivation—Guru devotion, cherishing the Dharma, and engaging in actual practice—Samantha's wisdom and compassion grew in leaps and bounds. In addition to offering divine guidance, counseling, and healing to help others, she offered her own living room every Saturday evening to other True Buddha practitioners for group practice. With her guidance and teaching, many people came to take refuge in Grand Master Lu and many others who had already taken refuge had their faith and confidence reinforced.

Obstacles in the Path of Cultivation

The path of cultivation is not an easy one and can be filled with challenges requiring creative solutions, as well as blessing and help from the Buddhas and Bodhisattvas. Early in her practice, Samantha encountered many obstacles that demanded skillful solutions and self-sacrifice. For example, there was a period during her early meditations when she saw demons trying to attack her. She was initially quite frightened and recited mantras and employed tantric implements such as vajra scepters to chase the demons away. The demons would recede momentarily, only to return fiercer than before. Finally, acting out of compassion, she experienced an epiphany. If her body was what the demons wanted to be happy, they could have it. Remaining completely detached and unperturbed, she conquered her fear. While in meditation she observed her body being cut up into pieces and carried away. Since then, the demons have never returned.

Another incident occurred in Redmond, WA while Samantha, her husband, a friend, and Megia (in one car), and her brother's family (in another car), were driving home from a Dharma ceremony. Grand Master suddenly appeared on the hood of Samantha's car, followed by the appearance of Maha Cundi Bodhisattva. She heard the voice of Maha Cundi reassuring her not to be afraid and to continuously recite the epithet Namo Maha Cundi Bodhisattva for help.

Samantha started to recite Cundi Bodhisattva's name. Suddenly Samantha felt her legs freeze and her hands completely paralyze on the steering wheel. Calmly and without fear, she felt a great force take over the car as it sped toward the center divider of the freeway. Just as the car approached the cement divider, a second mysterious force pulled the car back to the middle of the freeway. The first force attempted to maneuver the car toward the cement divider but the second force again pulled the car to the middle of the freeway. In this manner, the car swung back and forth in big zigzags several times before passing beyond the section of freeway with the cement center divide and finally coming to a stop at the side of the freeway. The other passengers had originally been asleep but were all awakened by the great forces and the zigzagging of the car. For many years, Andrew was reluctant to sit in a car driven by his wife.

During the Chinese New Year Blessing Ceremony in February 1987 conducted at Ling Shen Ching Tze by Grand Master, Samantha sincerely asked the Buddhas and Bodhisattvas to increase her wisdom. Suddenly, she experienced a great flame and heat surging up her middle channel all the way to her crown. Her kundalini had spontaneously awakened. The compassionate Buddhas and Bodhisattvas answered her prayer and Samantha was so moved by the experience that she broke down and cried from the depth of her whole being.

In May 1987, Samantha was instructed by Grand Master to establish the Purple Lotus Temple, a local chapter of the True Buddha School in the San Francisco Bay Area. In July of the same year, Samantha was formally ordained by Grand Master as a Vajra Master (Acharya) of the True Buddha School.

More Pregnancies

Shortly after Megia was born, Master Samantha heard a voice from above, saying "To the left is a dragon, to the right is a tiger, forming a tripod; the dragon head is descending." She was pregnant again. She guessed this time it would be a boy born in the year of the dragon. Later in a dream, she found herself inside a hospital where her newborn son was nowhere to be found. She heard a voice in the dream asking her where her daughter was, while another voice asked her to wait. Master Samantha did not understand the significance of the dream until the birth of her third child. This baby turned out to be a girl, Junia, instead of the boy she had anticipated.

One night when Junia was about two months old, Shakyamuni Buddha appeared to Master Samantha in the empty space emitting beams of red light on her and Andrew. Master Samantha realized that the vision signified another baby, yet she felt that her hands were already full with three children. She decided to have a tubal-ligation procedure and set up an appointment with her physician. But for one reason or another, important matters always came up at the last minute, so that she could not keep her appointments and had to reschedule. In the meantime, she found herself pregnant again. During this pregnancy, she had a premonition that she might not survive the childbirth. If this were so, she knew that it was her karma. Yet she was tortured by the thought of leaving Andrew and her small children. So, while making arrangements for her family if anything were to happen, she continued to immerse herself diligently and vigorously into her cultivation, often practicing with one baby on her back, one baby holding onto her, and still another growing inside her.

A Close Encounter with Death

On March 2, 1989, a son, Engih, was born to Samantha and Andrew. The delivery process was a smooth one. However, after the delivery, Master Samantha's blood pressure suddenly dropped and she went into shock. The doctors could not determine the source of the presumed internal blood loss, so they took Samantha into the operating room for exploratory surgery. As the nurses ran to bring more units of blood to the operating room for transfusion (she eventually required a total replacement of 6 liters of blood), Andrew knew that Samantha's life hung by a slender thread. In desperation he placed a phone call to the True Buddha Tantric Quarter in Redmond in the hopes of reaching Grand Master. Grand Master himself answered the phone. Andrew only managed to say that Samantha was in grave danger before breaking into uncontrollable sobs and hanging up the phone. At that hour, there was usually nobody present at the True Buddha Tantric Quarter. However, earlier that day there had been a snowstorm and Grand Master's car had stalled on his way home. For this reason he was spending the night at the True Buddha Tantric Quarter and thus was present to answer the phone. After Andrew hung up, Grand Master went to the shrine and remained in meditation throughout the night. He traveled out of his body to San Francisco to help Master Samantha.

When Samantha's spirit left her body that night, she felt immensely free. Looking down at her body on the surgical table, her abdomen open for examination by the surgeons, Samantha found that she did not want to go back. There was just too much pain and suffering in human existence. She focused on the practice that Grand Master had taught and on which she had worked so hard. She saw Kuan Yin, her Personal Deity, appearing. She was ready to merge with Kuan Yin when Grand Master appeared and blocked her way. Grand Master told her that her mission on earth was not yet accomplished and she would need to return to her body. Samantha, however, felt that the cross she had to bear, as a woman with so many small children, was just too hard and she begged Grand Master to let her go. She would rather come back reincarnated as a male and continue the service. Grand Master would not allow it. Samantha even tried to talk Grand Master into letting her go to the hell realm where she could serve Ksitigarbha in liberating the hell beings. However, Grand Master would not agree to that either. After much arguing, Samantha finally came back to the physical realm. Before she re-submerged into the human world, she visited the Maha Twin Lotus Ponds, the Pure Land of Padmakumara and experienced a taste of the Ocean of Consciousness of Vairocana Buddha (the merging with Universal Consciousness).

The surgery lasted a total of eight hours. The surgeons finally located the source of hemorrhage, a ruptured major blood vessel, and repaired it. After her near-death experience, Master Samantha felt deeply the limitations of the gross body and realized that the true significance of life is to raise one's spiritual consciousness and attain true awakening. She told herself that no matter what condition she found herself in, she would keep practicing to help sentient beings and spread the Dharma.

Service to the World

On May 2nd, 1987, Grand Master formally announced the establishment of Purple Lotus Temple and on July 22nd the same year conferred the title of Vajra Acharya to Master Samantha. During the last twenty years, besides serving as the residing master at the Purple Lotus Temple in San Bruno, California, Master Samantha has also traveled extensively around the world teaching the True Buddha Tantric Dharma. Places to which she has visited included Canada, Malaysia, Brunei, Taiwan, Hong Kong, Macau, China, Indonesia, Nepal, Thailand, Dominican Republic, Puerto Rico, Panama, Brazil, Japan, Singapore, Britain, Holland,

France, Australia and New Zealand. With the power she has developed through the practice of True Buddha Tantric Dharma, Master has rendered help to beings both in the living and bardo realms. So many miraculous occurrences have happened around Master Samantha that she is regarded by many people as a "Living Kuan Yin."

With great compassion, Master has worked indefatigably year round, providing personal consultations and public teachings, conducting meditation sessions, dharma ceremonies, fire pujas (totaling over 2000 since 1990), water pujas, and bardo services to benefit others. Over the last decade, many man-made or natural disasters have occurred. Master always conducted series of fire pujas over days to invoke Light to shine on the world to mitigate its sufferings. For example, when the energy crisis in California threatened to paralyze the state in 2001, Master and the students in PLT conducted 10 fire pujas invoking the Disaster Relief Tara to mitigate the crisis. After the 911 disaster, Master traveled to New York City to conduct bardo ceremonies for those perished in the terrorist attack. In 2003, Master conducted over one hundred ceremonies to mitigate the political storm threatening war between mainland China and Taiwan. After the South Asian Tsunami that struck in December 2004, Master and students of PLT engaged in a 19 hours marathon chanting of the Great Disaster Relief Mantra transmitted by our Guru to pray for expedition of relief to victims and to mitigate a potential plague that could affect hundreds of millions of people worldwide. Master also traveled to Aceh province in Indonesia, the hardest Tsunami hit area, in February 2005 to hold a dharma ceremony for 3000 people. Using the True Buddha Tantric Dharma method, Master helped the perished souls to eliminate fear and be reborn to the Pure Lands and also dedicated merits to the injured survivors so they could recover quickly and that relief and reconstruction could be accomplished smoothly.

During one of his early visits to the Purple Lotus Temple, Living Buddha Lian-sheng noted to Master Samantha the need to start a Buddhist education program. Consequently, she founded the Purple Lotus Buddhist School in Union City, California for kindergarten through twelfth grades in 1997 to fulfill that need. Besides offering a fully accredited academic curriculum, the school aims to nurture students to learn and practice enlightened living and thereby open their hearts and minds to develop the compassion, insight and skillful means to become responsible, benevolent and confident individuals dedicated to aiding all beings in handling life's challenges. In June 2007, PLBS proudly awarded diplomas to its fifth graduating class. All of the graduates have enrolled in universities or colleges, many in the University of California system.

Sacrificing her own personal and family life, Master often sleeps only a few hours a day, yet she is always energetic, gentle, patient, attentive to details, and caring. Although there may be a thousand things awaiting her decisions, she always gives the person seeking counsel in front of her total attention. Because of her ability to communicate with the many Buddhas and Bodhisattvas, her dharma talks are often filled with genuine wisdom teachings from the spiritual realm. What is most inspiring about Master Samantha is, however, her inviolate devotion to our guru Living Buddha Lian-sheng, serving as a most inspiring role model for many fellow True Buddha students who are also walking on the same pathway towards self-realization and enlighten-ment.

Chapter 1

On the Dharma Trip to Southeast Asia

*A talk by Master Samantha
at the Purple Lotus Temple
on March 17, 1990*

Good evening, fellow cultivators! For the past one and a half months, I have been traveling through Southeast Asia spreading the Buddhadharma. Today, I am very glad to be back here to see you again.

I'd like to report briefly on this Southeast Asia trip with our Guru. On the 20th of February, after the blessing ceremony in Singapore, I left our Guru and traveled on my own to give dharma teachings in Indonesia, Singapore, Taiwan, and Japan. Much took place during this time. First, let me recount the events at the four blessing ceremonies conducted by our Guru in Taiwan, Hong Kong, Malaysia, and Singapore. Apart from the many miraculous happenings, the one thing I feel really distinguishes our True Buddha School from other Buddhist schools is the full attendance at each of the four ceremonies.

In Taiwan, there are three contemporary Buddhist masters, Hsing Yun, Hui Lue, and our Guru, who can attract an attendance of more than ten thousand to their dharma ceremonies. So far, our Guru is the only one to have drawn that number of people to every ceremony he has held—any place, anytime, there is always a big turnout of people, coming of their own accord, to listen to the Buddhadharma. In Taiwan, perhaps it could be said that such events are not uncommon, as other masters have held ceremonies with turnouts over ten thousand. However, outside Taiwan, I dare say that there is no other Buddhist master who can match our Guru. None of our dharma ceremonies were accompanied by special advertising. If these ceremonies did not have their own appeal, people would not have attended. In Malaysia and Singapore, where the weather is very hot, the ceremonies were always full, regardless of the time of day they were held. Everyone stood outside under the blazing sun in 38 degree Celsius temperature (100 degrees Fahrenheit), from 4:00 p.m. to 10:30 p.m., for almost seven hours. Despite the cruelly hot weather, participants willingly bore the heat. I was deeply touched. To me this demonstrates the miraculous power of our Guru and the remarkableness of the True-Buddha School.

Different locations have different opening ceremony rituals. In Malaysia, where it is customary, lion dance performances welcomed our Guru and the other masters. It was a refreshing experience for me. We entered the ceremony hall led by two dancing lions amidst the noise of firecrackers. After a brief rest in the VIP lounge, we were treated to another round of celebration.

Seeing the throngs of people, with their attention focused on us, suddenly made it feel as if we were all participants in a stage play. Even the way of benefiting living beings had to be suited to the culture. The plot—spreading and transmitting the Buddhadharma—is repeated over and over, like an old movie continuously replayed. The actors continuously work as hard as they can, and the audience remains as involved as possible!

Next I would like to talk about our trip to Hong Kong. Perhaps you have already seen the pictures of the ghosts published in the 332nd issue of The Metropolitan Weekly, a Hong Kong magazine. Those pictures, taken during the Hong Kong Dharma Ceremony, caused much speculation, and I would like to give some explanation for those occurrences.

Last September, in 1989, when our Guru held a World Blessing and Deliverance Ceremony at the Hung Hom Stadium in Hong Kong, twelve thousand people attended, filling the stadium to capacity. It was the first time Hong Kong experienced a Buddhist organized ceremony of that size. It was so successful that some Buddhist organizations in Hong Kong became jealous and spiteful, and launched a vicious attack on our Guru after he left. They challenged the statements our Guru had made of seeing many spirits in attendance during the ceremony. Why was he the only one to have seen the ghosts? Who else had seen or heard them? Apart from commenting that all these things were impossible, they denounced him with harsh, vituperative language.

So on February 4th of this year, at the ceremony held at New Queen Elizabeth Stadium in Hong Kong, the same disembodied spirits who participated in last year's Blessing and Deliverance Ceremony appeared and spoke to our Guru, "Those human beings who do not believe in the existence of spirits are truly ignorant! To quiet their doubts and to vindicate you, we will give them definitive evidence of our existence."

That is the reason photographs of the headless ghost, the pale-faced ghost, and even the energy rays of dragon kings (nagarajas) were captured by audience members. The latter occurred during our Guru's transmission of the Dragon King Practice. Fifteen dragon kings came to take refuge in our Guru, resulting in the remarkable shots of energy rays in the form of dragons, descending one by one.

In order to determine the authenticity of these spiritual pictures, many specialists gathered together to study the negatives. After much argument, they finally confirmed that the negatives could not have been manufactured by any darkroom technique. As far as they could tell, the pictures with the transparent, disembodied, headless ghosts were legitimate. That is why they decided to publish the photographs on the cover of the 332nd issue of The Metropolitan Weekly with the following captions: "Strange Events at the Living Buddha's Blessing Ceremony," "Fierce Spirits Appear at the N.Q.E. Stadium with Photographs as Evidence."

Even more astonishing is this local Taiwanese magazine that I brought back. In it are also pictures of the headless ghost, the pale-faced ghost, and the dragon king rays. According to the magazine, these were photographed by their own reporters who could not explain the pictures. What a coincidence! Isn't it amazing?

The fifteen thousand people who participated during the February 10th ceremony in Malaysia also broke previous attendance records. During the ceremony someone photographed a greenish spirit. This greenish spirit was legless, with two arms extended, just like the kind of ghosts found in American cartoons—covered by a white bed sheet, with only two eyes showing, except that it was green. Of the two pictures developed, one showed the ghost flying in an arc in the air, and the other showed it prostrating in front of our Guru, paying homage. This was also a very unusual and amazing event. The local chapters of the True-Buddha School in Malaysia are going to send us those photographs. Those photographs were printed in the local newspapers there and have caused quite a stir.

Why were these ghosts and spirits photographed during the ceremonies? My personal opinion is as follows: Contemporary human beings are so mired in obscurations and ignorance that they take the illusory to be the substantial, and the unreal to be real. They no longer have the true wisdom of discernment. Without a method of practice and the teachings of a truly enlightened master, phenomena of higher realms are beyond their comprehension. Pictures of Buddha light are to them impossible and merely touch-ups created in dark rooms or results of improper exposure. When people refuse to believe in the existence of higher realms, an alternative method is to jolt them from their complacency and give them a glimpse of the lower, more terrifying realms. The purpose of these manifestations is to show those who refuse to be awakened, those who continually create negative karma, that ghosts do indeed exist. Because we live in a world of duality, if ghosts exist, then gods must exist too. Hopefully, with the acceptance of gods and ghosts, one will acknowledge and accept the Buddhist views of transmigration and the existence of the six realms. Beyond the six realms are the pure lands of the Buddhas and Bodhisattvas—states of absolute bliss and equality and freedom from eternal suffering.

So, if you take photographs such as these in the future, do not be frightened. It is all natural phenomena. One should instead be both cautious and grateful. Be cautious to avoid creating negative karma caused by being ignorant, and keep a clear mind focused on the path to liberation. Be grateful that you have the good fortune of encountering an enlightened master and be glad for the opportunity to receive teachings that will liberate you from suffering. Furthermore, congratulate yourself for seizing the opportunity to diligently cultivate and strive towards realization.

The ceremony on the 17th of February in Singapore, attended by eight thousand people, was also very sensational. The local newspapers all vied with one another to print their stories. At one point during the ceremony, our Guru told the audience that he would emit three rainbow lights and he asked the audience to snap photographs. Indeed, many captured the rainbow lights with their own cameras! The three rainbows formed a radiating arc, illuminating our Guru and the other masters. After such a public display of miracles, it is really a pity if people still refuse to believe!

After the ceremony in Singapore, our Guru departed for Seattle. Master Lian-zhi and I, however, upon invitation from the Indonesian chapter of the True Buddha School, Cin Siu Thang, traveled there. We were to attend their temple's consecration ceremony scheduled for the 23rd of February.

It should be noted at this point that Indonesia has a very stringent policy against anything Chinese in origin. Chinese books cannot be circulated freely and all symbols associated with the Chinese, such as dragons and phoenixes, are prohibited. Even Chinese writing in temples must be removed.

It was under these circumstances that I visited the temple of Master Ti Zheng. There I found, at the entrance of the Ksitigarbha Hall, a sign with its Chinese characters and images of a dragon and a phoenix covered over with paint. Our dharma brothers there use practice texts written in Indonesian because Chinese is forbidden. You can imagine the difficulty they go through to do this. Obtaining a copy of one of our Guru's books is like finding a piece of treasure. Everyone tries to make copies for circulation.

Because we came from overseas, we had to petition for a special permit in order to give public talks. Unfortunately, we were not granted the permit, so the local master Ti Zheng performed the rituals publicly while we used our powers of visualization for the empowerment and consecration steps. That day, four thousand people, including visitors and dharma brothers and sisters, attended the consecration ceremony. It was quite a spectacle.

Being warned of the possibility of imprisonment for giving public speeches without permits, Master Lianzhi and I could not accept speaking invitations at the various True Buddha chapters. My heart ached at the sight of the disappointed faces of our dharma brothers and sisters. The thought of ignoring the warning crossed my mind, but I would be jeopardizing the dharma brothers there if I were to be harassed and implicated in breaking the law. What if group cultivation is banned in the future as a result of this? Thus I remained steadfast and turned down their invitations to speak.

While many of our dharma brothers there were looking forward to our Guru's coming in June, there were many more who, after hearing the rumors and threats, were worried about possible riots that might ensue. These latter folk cited many reasons for dissuading him from coming, even suggesting that our Guru's personal safety might be in danger. As a result, many dharma brothers became extremely nervous about the whole event.

I view this matter differently. In the past I too would have worried as they did, but today, I no longer feel and think the same way. After my close encounter with death last March, I feel their concerns are quite unwarranted.

My personal belief is this: when those on the receptive end are ready, and when the time is right, our

Guru will travel where he is needed to teach, guide, and liberate, and a protective force will spontaneously envelop the region. Such has been the case at every ceremony held thus far. No man-made obstructions have prevented them. When the karma of a certain region is ripe, our Guru will travel there. Fear of riots, government instability and natural disasters arise because people do not understand the causes behind these events.

Those with wisdom, under such circumstances, will seek blessing and guidance from an enlightened, Living Buddha. A ceremony led by our Guru will bring empowerment and the blessing of the Buddhas and Bodhisattvas to the area. Not only will natural and man-made disasters disappear, but peace, harmony, and stability will reign.

I know my view may be different from others. I am aware that our Guru's personal safety must be protected, but I also understand that a realized Buddha knows more than we do. The events of his life exist for a reason. Take for example, Mala Maudgalyayana, one of the ten chief disciples of Shakyamuni Buddha. His supreme miraculous power enabled him to escape many disasters in life, yet in the end, he allowed himself to be stoned to death. Why? Because he knew that it was his karma and an event he was not meant to escape.

I privately told the dharma brothers that, should our Guru encounter any unfortunate events, it would be fate and karma. There was no need to worry. The sowing of Buddhism must take precedence over all else. Our

Guru himself casts aside concern for his own life and safety and has dedicated his life to the deliverance of sentient beings, even if it means he will be smashed to smithereens. Once the karma of a certain region ripens, and it is time for him to go there, no amount of opposition can stop him!

It is no surprise that we are facing many difficulties in obtaining an official permit for our Guru's public teaching in June. The authorities are very worried because our Guru's students and followers comprise the largest percentage of Indonesia's Buddhist population. It is understandable that the officials would want to make things difficult for us. They have raised numerous obstacles, including one request to provide definitive proof of the existence of the Maha Twin Lotus Ponds. How indeed shall we prove that Maha Padmakumara came from the Western Paradise of Ultimate Bliss? Is there a witness? Is there any evidence in the Buddhist Canon?

Master Ding Zhi-fang, the organizer for the ceremony, decided to purchase a copy of the Buddhist Canon from Hong Kong and have it transported to Indonesia. Even as we speak, over a hundred disciples are searching daily through the scriptures to find this reference for the authorities. Does it exist? Of course! The act of reading through these Buddhist scriptures is a meritorious endeavor. Finding this reference will establish a position for our True Buddha School in the future. Truly the proof is there, not just in Buddhist literature, but also in the classics of Taoism.

Our Guru has told us that the existing Buddhist Canon is an incomplete collection of Buddha's teachings. There are many as yet unseen teachings stored in the Palace of the Dragon King. Our Guru has visited and read those teachings in his meditations, and in the future, he will write them down. Shakyamuni Buddha was the first one to visit the Dragon Palace, followed by Nagarjuna. Our Guru, Living Buddha Lian-sheng, is the third. The events of today are results of our generation's karma. The True Buddha School was created to fulfill this need and its task is to publicize the true dharma. Undoubtedly our Guru will eventually add more chapters to the Buddhist Canon. For now, however, the dharma brothers in Indonesia are searching through what we have, and the evidence will eventually be revealed.

There is a Tibetan book published in Hong Kong with drawings of mandalas and various Buddhas and Bodhisattvas. The dates of the original drawings are unknown but were created from memory by numerous high lamas who had seen the mandalas in their meditations. I have seen this book and in it is a page of the Great Assembly of Padmakumaras. The mandala clearly depicted on the drawing has been in existence for a long time. In preparation for the June ceremony, this book has been sent to Indonesia.

There are many other examples in existence. In many antique shops, people have seen standing statues of

Padmakumara holding the Preaching Mudra in one hand and a white lotus in the other. The antique dealers call these images Lotus Bodhisattva instead of Padmakumara. Both terms actually bear the same meaning: Innocence and Purity. There is another statue that holds the same Preaching Mudra and lotus and wears the same garments but is called Amitabha instead of Padmakumara. All these statues represent the same being. Many such proofs are surfacing because the time is ripe. Our Guru has entered the third phase of his life: wandering the world to deliver sentient beings. During this phase, evidence will gradually surface to help the people of this world better understand and accept the establishment of the True Buddha School.

Next, I would like to discuss my impressions of Indonesia. Upon our arrival at the Indonesian airport, we were led directly to the VIP lounge without any problems. After leaving the airport, we drove through the streets of Jakarta in a luxurious sedan. Every time our car slowed or stopped, hawkers (adults as well as children) surrounded us, knocking at the windows, trying to sell us all kinds of magazines from the United States and Hong Kong. They were sweating under the blazing sun, dressed in dirty, tattered clothes. Being unaccustomed to such a scene, I could not help but glance at them. When they noticed this, however, they would crowd around even closer. Our driver warned us to make sure all windows were shut and to avoid eye contact, otherwise we would never be able to get away.

As I witnessed all this, I was suddenly overcome by an acute awareness of the inequalities of life. As we sat in the comfort of our air-conditioned luxury sedan, the people outside had to endure the scorching heat, struggling, sweating, just to sell a few magazines, flowers, or soda-pop so they could buy their next mouthful of rice. The contrast was so staggering that a surge of unrest and sadness welled up inside me.

Later we stopped by a department store to pick up a few items and when we came out, it was pouring rain. In front of the store were many small children with umbrellas in their hands, trying to make some money. We did not want to get wet, so we waved them over and immediately, twenty or thirty small children rushed over, all fighting to offer their services. I did not know how I could shield myself at the same time with 20 to 30 umbrellas, so I had to make a selection. Randomly I picked a little boy, about 6 or 7 years old, who only reached up to my waist. His umbrella was turned up at one corner and half of it seemed to be flying away. Because he was so short, he had to stand on tip toe to hold up the umbrella for me while he himself got drenched. I, of course, was also getting wet because an overturned umbrella could not really shield me from the rain.

When we returned to our car, I retrieved some money from my purse to pay him and one of the dharma sisters told me that a hundred Indonesian dollars was the customary fee. I handed him the money, and after saying "terminakasih" (thank you), he dashed back to the crowd, his umbrella in his hand, looking for another customer.

My first question to the dharma sister after getting into the car was, "How much U.S. is a hundred Indonesian dollars?" "A nickel," she replied. Only a nickel! I felt really bad that I had given him so little money. We are both human beings, yet our lives are so different. I thought to myself, "He had to brave the rain for a nickel to buy a meal. Despite getting soaked, he still prays for rain, because without it, he doesn't even get the chance to make a little money."

In the evening, we were taken out for dinner. The food was exquisite with gourmet dishes such as shark fin soup and abalone. So much was ordered that we could not eat it all. I asked them the cost for a banquet such as this, and was told, "U.S. $150." Oh! One hundred fifty U.S. dollars! Then I inquired into the average living standards in Indonesia and was told that, in general, it was very low. Many Indonesians could not afford to eat at restaurants. One could hire a local for household help, seven days a week, with no days off, for twenty US dollars a month. Listening to all this, my heart was deeply touched.

Traveling around the world has enabled me to further comprehend the worries and ignorance of living beings. All of you here today are people with great blessings. We are assured of our next meal. Even if we may not be among the extremely rich, we do not worry about living from day to day. We can practice Buddhism openly, meditate, or study the sutras as we choose. We do not worry about meeting our basic needs—food, clothing, shelter—nor about censorship of certain spoken and written languages. We are indeed very fortunate and very blessed!

Indonesia has a population of one billion. There are people everywhere, and the majority of them are very poor. When will they have the opportunity to listen to the Buddhadharma, take refuge in an enlightened master, or do cultivations that will lead to liberation? When will they cease to suffer the pain of retribution, ignorance, and transmigration?

The money spent by one person on a single meal is equivalent to hours of hard work for another. If holding umbrellas in the rain brings in a nickel per sale, it will take three thousand sales to make one hundred fifty dollars. How can we help these people? How can we relieve their suffering? How can we all achieve equality and non-discrimination?

Only the Buddhadharma can genuinely liberate and deliver them. We must teach that to avoid retribution, we must first stop committing unwholesome actions. Taking refuge in an enlightened master, cultivating the correct practice, repenting for one's wrongs, and performing good deeds will lead one to freedom from the pain of transmigration. I hope you all can do your best to spread Buddhism and tell everyone about the True Buddha Vajrayana Cultivation. All it takes is one person spreading the word to ten, ten spreading the word to a hundred, a hundred to a thousand, and pretty soon everyone will get to hear and practice it. Eventually a refreshing realization will clear people's minds.

Next, let me relate to you some of the miracles that took place while I was in Indonesia. One of our dharma brothers living in Bandung by the name of Chang Yin-yuan has a wife, Li Yi-mei, who was afflicted with an illness known as "the flying snake syndrome." She had bouts of attacks during which she would experience extreme weakness and excruciating headaches. After I was informed of her illness, I paid her a visit at their home where she was bedridden, very pale, weak, and unable to move her limbs. I immediately went into concentration to invoke Kuan Yin Bodhisattva and our Guru, Living Buddha Lian-sheng. While forming the Nine-True-Words Mudra, I recited a mantra, and visualized our Guru together with all the Buddhas and Bodhisattvas compassionately shining light on her. I blessed her and transmitted energy to her head and her whole body.

Afterwards, I formed the purification boundary around her house and promised that I would conduct deliverance ceremonies for the next four days and dedicate the merits to her creditors in the spirit realm. Master Lian-zhi also stayed at their house to help conduct the ceremonies.

That night, while writing the evocation edict that would formally start the deliverance ceremony, the entire house became inhabited by spirits! All around us, spirits were gathering. Master Lian-zhi came downstairs, calling me, "Hurry up, hurry up! They are all here! I saw the stuffed birds in the specimen case flapping their wings. A Malaysian lady spirit in Mrs. Zhang's room was silently waving her hand. And their ancestors, whose photographs are hanging on the walls, are coming out one by one! Hurry Up!" While continuing to write the edict (a.k.a. prayer of intent), I replied, "Be patient, it's almost done." All this time I could see numerous snakes crawling on the floor. A sudden chill pervaded the house as the spirits grew increasingly impatient. Finally, with all the preparatory work done, we began the deliverance ceremony. Master Lian-zhi and I conducted in unison the Mahamudra for Deliverance taught by our Guru. Spirits, many of them stained with blood, poured into the home. The next day one of the dharma sisters, Lian-yuk, informed us that nearby was a public cemetery where Indonesian Chinese, murdered during an anti-Chinese riot thirty years ago, were buried.

The day after the deliverance ceremony, Mrs. Zhang was able to get out of bed and move around the house. She was able to sleep well for the first time in a long while, ending a long period of chronic insomnia. The second day she began doing light housework. After the fourth day, she resumed all her regular activities.

Our schedule was so full during this trip that each night we would not be done until about 9:30. Master Lian-zhi, who is not as strong and robust as I am, would

39

go to bed as soon as we arrived home. Being a nurse made a great deal of difference in the way she took care of herself. She was very disciplined. If food did not agree with her, she would not eat it. When she was tired, she slept. I, on the other hand, will eat anything and tend to stay up even when it is late. It is hard for me to stop and rest even when I am really tired. If I keep this up, she is surely going to outlive me!

On the second night, as was her custom, Master Lian-zhi went straight to bed after we arrived home. After our exhausting day, the temptation was just too great to resist. Watching her sleep, I could not keep my body going. I squinted at my watch, taking note of the time, 9:30. "Okay, let me rest a little and at eleven o'clock sharp I will conduct the deliverance ceremony." I must have fallen asleep as soon as I finished saying this.

One dharma sister, Lian-shang, had heard about the deliverance ceremony the first day and was afraid to come over. After learning from us the second day that Mrs. Zhang had markedly improved, she decided to join us. While we were upstairs fast asleep, Lian-shang was downstairs chatting with Lian-yuk.

Not too long after I fell asleep, I was awakened by knocks at the door. I arose to open the door and when Lian-shang saw me she replied, "Oh! You were asleep! I thought you had started already." "No, why is that?" I asked. She then explained, "I heard someone beating the gong three times! I looked at my watch and it was eleven o'clock, so I thought you had started the deliverance ceremony without me. That's why I came running up to join you. But you were not in the shrine room when I got there. And here I've found you both asleep in the bedroom." She continued, "How strange! Where did the gong sound come from? We all heard it!"

Master Lian-zhi replied, "Oh, the old monk is here already. An old monk from the spirit realm has also come to help us with the deliverance ceremony!"

"Eleven o'clock sharp. How punctual!" I said.

Lian-shang never did figure out where the gonging had come from.

On the third day, our schedule was just as busy. When we arrived home, Master Lian-zhi, exhausted, again went to rest on her bed. (Lian-shang had not been feeling well that day and had come back to Mrs. Zhang's house earlier to rest.) Seeing Master Lian-zhi sound asleep, I was again tempted. I mentally told the spirits, "All right, eleven o'clock. I will conduct the deliverance ceremony at eleven o'clock." Immediately, I fell asleep.

A short while later, I was again awakened by knocking at the door. Opening the door, I again found Lian-shang, who uttered, "You two are still sleeping! I was sound asleep too, but for some reason, a force kept pulling me off the bed. Half asleep, I turned over twice, ignoring it, but it kept dragging me until after the third time, I finally woke up. Then I looked at the clock—it was eleven, time for the deliverance ceremony. That's why I came running up again to join you! Really I had no idea that you two were still sound asleep!"

The final day, after finishing the deliverance ceremony, Master Lian-zhi and I stayed up to chat. While we were talking, I noticed by my bedside a spirit who had been staring silently at us, dressed in the attire of an official of the Qing Dynasty.

After being stared at for a while, I began feeling uneasy, so I asked Master Lian-zhi if she noticed him too. She said she had not been paying attention and had not noticed him. After a while, however, she exclaimed, "Oh, yes, you are right! Right over there in that corner! He has been there for several days already."

"That's right. Him standing over my bed like that, makes it difficult for me to sleep in certain positions," I complained. "I don't like it this way. I'll just establish a Vajra Boundary around my bed." Standing up, I proceeded to form the mudra as rays of light surged forth. The Qing Dynasty official immediately backed up into a corner of the room, appearing very scared. He shouted, "I don't mean any harm at all. Don't be angry! I really don't have any bad intentions."

"Really? Then why are you standing over my bed disturbing us?" I asked.

He replied, "I was just admiring you. There is no harm in that."

"When I am sleeping, I don't want to be disturbed. If you want to look, you can do that during the day. At night, I am sorry, but I don't appreciate being looked at!" Then, seeing how sorry he was, I thought to myself, "Well, as long as he is not doing any harm and

42

not being disruptive, I will tolerate his staring." We decided not to be bothered anymore by his presence.

As cultivators, we should realize that we cannot always do whatever we want just because we think no one is watching. We are surrounded by many invisible beings, some from higher or lower realms, and they know everything we do. This is absolutely true. Do not think you are alone when you sleep for there may be a circle of beings watching and admiring you! You are simply not aware of them! If you can feel their presence, they are everywhere. The boundary between the living and the dead is a thin line.

As a child, I had heard about a lady living in our neighborhood who, after having narrowly survived an auto accident, appeared to go crazy. Everyone said that she was mentally ill. When she "died" and was revived, her third eye spontaneously opened. Why did everyone think she was so changed? Wherever she walked, she would zigzag, as if she was afraid to bump into someone. Often, she was heard apologizing as if she had bumped into someone. When her husband drove, she would exclaim nervously, "Oh! You just hit someone!" At the time, I too thought she was crazy. But now I realize she had been seeing spirits everywhere. That is why she was trying to avoid bumping into them.

After the restoration of Mrs. Zhang's health, many people heard of the news and invited me over to help them. One individual was an old gentleman with liver cancer. After exhausting the treatments of many

Western and Chinese-herbal doctors, he was still sick. He experienced multiple bouts of diarrhea every day and had been bedridden for seven to eight months.

His son wanted me to go to his house to see him, but it was almost midnight at the time, and the house was an hour away by car. So, I asked him if his father could come to us instead. "How can he?" he replied. "He has not been able to move for almost 7 or 8 months now! That would not be possible."

Looking at the time again, I told him, "I will go tomorrow then. You can help him now by taking refuge for him. Do not postpone this. It is important that he do this. Visualize your father in front of you taking refuge." The son also signed up to take refuge himself.

Another individual wanted to sign his daughter up to take refuge. His daughter, who was ten months old, had lost her appetite and was having bouts of diarrhea six to seven times each day.

There were many people that night asking to take refuge in our Guru. I told all of them to press their palms together with sincerity, and, for those who had signed up relatives and friends, to also visualize them by their side receiving the empowerment. After the empowerment, I told each one of them to make a wish. Then, as I rang the Vajra bell to bless the list of names of people who had just taken refuge, a brilliant red beam descended from the sky, and I heard a very clear announcement from the Buddhas and Bodhisattvas: "All the wishes made today will be fulfilled." I immediately related this message to all present.

The next day, I went to visit the old gentleman with cancer. Surprisingly, he was already out of bed and walking around! His son told me that since taking refuge the day prior and after drinking the preparation from the "fu", the spiritual paper charm, his father was able to get up, move, and take a meal!

When I returned home, I found the father of the ten month old daughter who had taken refuge the night before, waiting for me, saying, "My daughter ate a big meal today and stopped having diarrhea for the first time in months after taking refuge and drinking the preparation from the paper charm you wrote. It is just miraculous!"

Incidents like these are many. The people who came back all reportedly improved. The miracles were endless!

All these are powerful evidence and proof that the True Buddha Dharma taught by our Guru is, indeed, real. The True Buddha School established by him is real, and everything about Living Buddha Lian-sheng is real. He is, indeed, a Great Buddha incarnated because of his compassion and vows. In order to deliver living beings throughout this world, he has set up many expedient ways to lead the lost, and to help the confused living beings to return to the Source. Innumerable beings will be delivered this way! If we could only understand how remarkable this Dharma is, we would truly treasure it.

We would seize the opportunity to spread the good news to the lost and the confused, so they will all come to take refuge! Do not procrastinate—do not delay your cultivation any longer! Living Buddha Lian-sheng has come for the One Great Cause! Bring out your hearts! If you truly wish to help and aid other people, do not waste any more time. Time will not stand still for us! We must speak and act now. Only then will we truly liberate all living beings from suffering!

Om Mani Padme Hum.

Chapter 2

On Reincarnation and Cultivation

*A talk by Master Samantha
at Lei Zang Buddhist Temple,
Alhambra, California
on November 16, 1990*

Fellow cultivators and visitors, good evening!

As we all know, today is the birthday of Medicine Buddha. What a wonderful coincidence that I am able to celebrate this event with everyone present. Celebration of Medicine Buddha's birthday can help us reduce and eradicate karmic hindrances accumulated by our body, mind, and speech through ignorance. Earlier, we recited Medicine Buddha's twelve great vows. I was so moved by those vows that a profound feeling of gratitude welled up within me. I could feel His devotedness and compassion very strongly. Medicine Lapis Lazuli Light Buddha together with all the Buddhas and Bodhisattvas, in their compassion, have generated such great vows to liberate all sentient beings. It is just remarkable!

As we were reading Medicine Buddha's Original Vows and Merits Sutra, I saw Medicine Lapis Lazuli Light Buddha appear in the Empty Space. His crystal clear body radiated a strong blue light over everyone. I knew then that everyone present is very blessed. Blessings from Medicine Lapis Lazuli Light Buddha increase fortune and wisdom. Our sincerity in celebrating his birthday will reduce and prevent many inauspicious events, including imminent calamities. Such is the merit and efficacy in participating in today's ceremony and meditation.

Next I would like to thank the Lei Zang Temple of Los Angeles for inviting me here to meet and speak with you. This has actually not been a simple matter.

When I was first invited here at the beginning of last year, I was very pregnant and unable to come. Then, on the second of March last year, I had a profound and transformative experience. After giving birth, I began hemorrhaging. I hemorrhaged for almost four and a half hours. I lost most of my body's blood and needed transfusions. Not only that, my consciousness departed from my physical body and left the human realm. Were it not for our Guru, who traveled out of his body to save me and bring me back, I would not be sitting here with all of you today.

All those present today are extremely blessed. I say this because we all have the wisdom and opportunity to uphold and practice the True Buddha Tantric Dharma. This affinity has brought us together, and we can all continue our path of cultivation until we reach our Home—the Maha Twin Lotus Ponds. Our Guru led me back from the realm of Western Paradise to bear witness to the events I encountered and to let everyone know that the Maha Twin Lotus Ponds—the Pure Land of Amitabha—exists. Only by taking refuge in the True Buddha School, by practicing the True Buddha Tantric Dharma, and by becoming a True Buddha practitioner, can we return to the Maha Twin Lotus Ponds, our place of origin.

Each of us originated there, so why are we here? Through continuous transmigration, we experience a diversity of roles, each one urging us on to successfully complete our mission.

Our presence today, sitting here in harmony amidst our differences, is a testament to this. This affinity is not easily perceived. How many generations past and how many eons were needed for this affinity to mature? If you understand the principle of cause and effect, karma, as explained by the Buddhadharma, you will not find this affinity surprising. Although we are all derived from the same source, the actions created by our various division bodies result in the formation of unique affinities with those around us. At the Purple Lotus Temple, I have said to the dharma brothers and sisters, "Notice the people around you—those in front of you, behind you, to your right and to your left. They may have been your fathers, mothers, brothers, sisters, husbands, and wives in previous lives. We do not realize that we are all from the same source because we only see others as they are in this lifetime. In previous lives, we were husbands, wives, sons and daughters, brothers and sisters. Our pasts are intertwined."

Our worldly life is very short; the years pass by very quickly. The familial affinities formed in one lifetime do not last forever. Once your physical body and consciousness depart, you will reincarnate according to your karma. You will form new affinities and new families. When this happens, will you recognize your families and relatives from past lives? No. You will have donned a new mask, a new name, and be in a new environment. You have already forgotten your place of origin.

On Reincarnation and Cultivation

How many times have you reincarnated? How many eons have you suffered? Our planet, Earth, has already experienced seven waves of destruction. How long does it take Earth to repeat each cycle of formation, existence, decay, and destruction? Why do we keep returning? I have often contemplated this question—what is the most painful experience in life? It is not the agony of human relationships, but the continuous reincarnation into one role after another—from infancy to old age—cycling over and over.

We are a result of our previous actions. Because of ignorance, we succumb to greed, lust, and pride. What costs have we paid to fill our need for earthly pleasures—beautiful villas, luxurious sedans, a gentle wife, a caring husband, obedient children, fame, and success? Are you aware of life's impermanence?

Three years ago I was at the Los Angeles airport with my daughter, Megia. I had just given a talk at the Mui Yin Society and we were waiting for our flight back to San Francisco. While waiting, I saw a dignified gentleman and an elegant lady chatting with one another. They were sitting beside us so I could not help but overhear their conversation. The gentleman was talking about his big home, his prosperous business, how his children all attending Stanford were getting A's... Wow! Everything was so picture perfect! As I cast another glance at them, I could not help but wonder what a person in his shoes could possibly ask for. I envied him and even fantasized about my future successes.

Soon after boarding instructions were announced, I got up to walk around. I had only taken a few steps when I heard a loud crash behind me. As I turned, I saw the gentleman previously sitting next to me sprawled on the floor. His glasses had broken into fragments, cutting his eyes, as blood flowed down his face. He had urinated, possibly due to shock of the fall on his bladder. The color of his face had turned from pink to white. Then his breathing stopped—a heart attack?—as he lay on the floor next to my feet. Holding my baby in my arms, I was shaking all over. In my heart, I was crying, "Why is this happening? Why is this happening?" Suddenly the phrase *all phenomena in life are impermanent* entered my mind. In that one moment, I experienced the meaning of impermanence. Where was his business? Where was his money? His family? His prestige? Where had this man gone to now? He could no longer be found in this world. The shock I experienced from witnessing the event was profound. The instant he fell by my feet, my fantasies and dreams were shattered.

When I returned to San Francisco, I continued to ponder the true meaning of life in this world. If you understand the relationship between karma and transmigration, you will not be troubled by the relationships and affinities formed in this lifetime.

Every person is born at a certain hour, on a certain day, on a certain month, in a certain year. The time of one's birth dictates one's fate and one's karma. The family into which one is born and one's surname are predetermined. One bears the fruits of past lifetime actions. This cannot be avoided. However, through spiritual cultivation and accumulation of charitable and virtuous deeds, one can change one's fate.

Ever since I was a child, my mother would obtain divinations for me. It was predicted that I would meet a bloody calamity last year. I do not know how much money she spent in obtaining those readings, but last year, I faced my close encounter with death. It was my karma, the fruit of my actions from a previous life. There was no escaping it. Otherwise, Maudgalyayana, one of the ten chief disciples of Shakyamuni Buddha, noted especially for his miraculous power, would not have been stoned to death. Surely, with his miraculous powers, he could have run away from this retribution. But for how long could he run? It was only fair to reveal his karma to sentient beings. It would warn them to stop creating negative karma for themselves.

So last year I faced my pre-determined calamity. Fortunately, a few years before, I had found my way to the correct path and took refuge in a truly illuminated Guru.

I often tell people that, if one is to take refuge, one should do so through a truly Enlightened Master, not just any master with fame. A truly Enlightened Master will eradicate ignorance, enable one to reveal the light from within, and guide one on a path to Eternal Liberation. This must be recognized.

I myself have received much empowerment and guidance from our Guru. When I read our Guru's books on spiritual experiences, it is not to collect the different meditation methods he teaches, but to find his motives for writing these books. What is he trying to teach us? What can readers and disciples learn from each book? I myself have gleaned a great deal from his books over the last several years. I followed our Guru, took a few steps along the path, and prepared to depart (from this physical existence). But before I could do so, our Guru blocked my departure. Perhaps I had not moved fast enough! This time my goal is to work harder in my practice, so that he will not catch me again!

Returning to this human life has made me realize that this path is not easy. The most difficult thing about being human is not knowing one's purpose in life. It is actually quite easy to be awakened if we stick to the path. Despite knowledge of this, we allow ourselves to fall prey to the many external temptations that hinder us from awakening. Materialistic traps only serve to entangle us—from childhood to adulthood, from adulthood to senility, we constantly compete for more and more acquisitions. The more we desire, the more trouble we have, and the more suffering we encounter. Then at the moment of death, everything is dropped and we return to the original state of possessing nothing.

Each one of you is here today because of a desire to walk on the path of cultivation. There are many factors preventing us from completely embracing the path, but as long as we have the desire, we need not be discouraged. Do not be afraid of storms and obstructions that arise along the path. With simply the desire to return Home, we will surely find the methods to lead us there. Rest your desires on the path of cultivation, and we will surely return to our Original Home, the Maha Twin Lotus Ponds.

Om Mani Padme Hum.

Chapter 3

Bodhicitta

A talk by Master Samantha
at the Purple Lotus Temple
on February 29, 1992

The Support of Jambhala

I recall that it was on a Saturday, January 7th, 1989 when the Purple Lotus Temple's weekly group cultivation moved from the small living room of my apartment to the Masonic Temple in San Mateo. That evening we were to conduct the Yellow Jambhala Practice. I remember vividly that, during that particular meditation, Yellow Jambhala manifested and scattered piles of cash, in American currency, from the sky. All that money spread like a net descending over everyone's head. Such a vision was a first in my Jambhala practices.

Among all the cultivators in the audience, I noticed a particularly high pile of cash scattered over one dharma brother, and on top of that pile, a huge diamond of several thousand carats had landed on his head.

At that moment, Yellow Jambhala commented, "As long as one generates the bodhicitta and vows to uphold the Buddhadharma, one will obtain this money."

After the meditation, I told the audience of the vision I had, but I did not disclose the one dharma brother upon whom the pile of money had descended. After all, the generation of bodhicitta should come voluntarily and sincerely from the bottom of one's heart. These actions cannot be forced nor should they be carried out "reluctantly."

Yellow Jambhala has declared, "As long as one upholds the Buddhadharma, I will surely support him."

This money has already manifested itself upon my fellow cultivators and is ready to materialize anytime, even though it cannot be seen with human eyes. How does one receive this money then? To which bank does one go? What is the account number to access this money?

I have been paying particular attention to the dharma brother with the exceptionally high pile of money dropped on him because, at that time, Yellow Jambhala also revealed, "If this person devotes himself to the propagation of the Buddhadharma, he will make three million dollars in four years." I attempted to give this man some hints, but he failed to perceive them. Finally, I encouraged him to do more charitable deeds, although I still did not tell him directly, "There is a lot of money sitting above you, just waiting to come through!"

The truth is, if one voluntarily commits oneself to the upholding of the Buddhadharma, the Buddhas and Bodhisattvas will surely make one a channel by which money comes through to help the sentient beings. When people generate bodhicitta and commit to support various platforms for cultivation, the Buddhas and Bodhisattvas will continue to send money their way.

True Bodhicitta

One of our students in Los Angeles is in the real estate business. When he opened his first office, his financial situation was very tight. Yet even under such circumstances, this student was still very supportive of the Buddhadharma. With minimal funds, he could only afford a very small corner of advertisement in a booklet of real estate ads, and the last copy of that edition was unfortunately tossed on the street after which it began raining. The booklet became wet and dirty after it was trampled on by pedestrians.

Someone, however, happened to walk by that day and seeing the dirty copy of advertisements, casually picked it up and took it home. Flipping through the booklet, a small framed advertisement caught his eye and he called up this student of ours. Today, this individual is the biggest customer and best friend of our dharma brother.

This dharma brother told me the following, "Many things are not accomplished by our efforts alone. I am merely a channel for the Buddhas and Bodhisattvas." He sincerely believed that if the Buddhas and Bodhisattvas had not wanted to use him as a channel, he would not have been as successful and prosperous in his business.

I tried to convince my husband, Andrew, to make this commitment: "I will offer one third of my annual income to Master Samantha, without any strings attached, for the propagation of the dharma."

After listening, Andrew immediately took out a calculator and started computing. He shook his head, "That won't work! If I gave you one third of my gross income, the remainder would not be enough to cover salaries, raw materials, and other household expenses!"

I explained to him, "This is actually a matter of whether or not you can truly generate bodhicitta. With the right understanding and knowledge, if you do not harbor fear and doubt, if you walk ahead courageously, channels will naturally open up for you. The Buddhas and Bodhisattvas, the various deities and dharma protectors, will manifest to support you because your work is for the benefit of sentient beings and not for the satisfaction of selfish desires. Besides, my work is not confined locally. I will be bringing your money to all parts of the world to sow the seeds of the Buddhadharma, to generate more affinities between the many sentient beings and the dharma. I am helping them take refuge so they might cultivate to liberate themselves from their burdens. This is work of infinite merits!"

I continued, "But, all this depends on the generation of bodhicitta from within. If you do not have this understanding and knowledge, do not force the good will. If you do, once challenges arise, you will lose your faith and give up."

Many people will perform a few charitable deeds when obstacles arise then complain, "Oh! Why am I still facing these problems after all the charity I have done?" They start to find fault with their actions, and because of lack of true understanding, they lose faith and the will to cultivate.

In actuality, all charitable deeds and merits accumulated are for oneself and no one can take them away. This can be likened to the intake of food—after one opened one's mouth to eat and swallow food, who can take it away? If one understands the meaning of charity, one knows that, by giving to others, one is actually giving to oneself. The process of giving is actually training the heart for infinite expansion. The more you give, the freer you will become. Sentient beings are constrained by "self-contraction." If they can release this "self-contraction," the Infinite Heart will manifest and obstructions will automatically subside. This is why those who give are blessed. To give is to receive more within. One will no longer feel the need to argue over trifle matters. One's vision and state of mind will expand. Without fear and attachments, calm, stability, and peace arise. Thus, the individual who generates bodhicitta to perform charitable acts, ultimately is the one who benefits.

A True Cultivator

Charity is not limited to the act of donating money. At the Purple Lotus Temple, if one notices that the carpet or altar is wet or dirty, one can help clean up. If flowers on the altar have withered, snip them off or water them. All these are acts of charity. People who understand the meaning of charity will be charitable anytime, anywhere.

Earlier someone downstairs had spilled some water on the floor and everyone simply walked around it. When I went downstairs to look after the children, I saw the water on the floor and immediately went to get paper towels to wipe up the spill. A dharma sister saw me and exclaimed, "Oh! Master, why are you the one cleaning up the floors?"

Why not? Am I not a practitioner? What jobs are meant for particular people, and for whom should one wait to get something done?

What place is not suitable for cultivation? It would be wrong to assume that one can only cultivate at the Purple Lotus Temple where there are the enshrinements of the Buddhas. People who truly understand, seize every moment to cultivate. At a department store, if one sees a piece of clothing on the floor, one can pick it up and put it back on a hanger. If one sees fruit peelings on the floor, one can pick them up and toss them into the trash can. These are very trivial matters, but when one has kindness in one's heart, such actions naturally become habit. I once went into a restroom and noticed everyone immediately pinching their noses and exiting one of the stalls after walking in. I went in and found the toilet stopped up by wads of toilet paper with pieces of feces floating at the top of the toilet bowl. When I saw this, I very naturally put my hand into the water to pull out those paper towels and dispose of them. I then flushed the toilet and went to wash my hands. If it is not my job, whose job is it?

For example, in public restrooms, if the counter is wet, casually grab some papers towels and dry it. This will make it more pleasant for the next person, so he or she will not have to wet their clothes. Yes, these are very trivial matters, but as cultivators, we are working continuously to correct our speech and actions.

To understand true cultivation is to realize that there is no place on this earth that is not a platform for cultivation. One does not just practice here in front of the altar, but everywhere. Wherever you are, whatever you are doing, visualize the Buddhas and Bodhisattvas sitting above your head, emanating light, and mentally chant mantras. If one's mind harbors no thought of filth, one will not feel dirty, even if holding excrement in one's hands.

People who know how to cultivate will give of themselves and form good affinities with others wherever they go. People who do not know how to cultivate will constantly be thinking of ways to take from others and gain more for themselves.

I am not asking you to give up your respon-sibilities as a human being but to practice opening your heart. Once your heart is open, you will understand the meaning of life and the emptiness of all material things. What is it that belongs to you eternally? It can never be anything in the material realm.

Contemplate and understand this: What is cultivation? Who should be doing the job?

Om Mani Padme Hum.

Chapter 4

Reflections on "Birthdays"

A talk by Master Samantha Chou
at the Purple Lotus Temple
on January 30, 1993.

Reflections on "Birthdays"

Master Samantha, over the past several years, has traveled extensively to teach the Dharma. Her teachings have taken her outside of the San Francisco Bay Area, and due to her extensive travels, there has never been any celebration of her birthday at the Purple Lotus Temple. Therefore, the students at PLS decided to give her a surprise birthday celebration. This took place after the usual Saturday group cultivation on January 30, 1993, as she was soon to travel to Calgary, Canada to spread the Dharma. The following is an excerpt of her teaching given that day.

I would like to thank everyone for this birthday celebration. Some of you have asked me to share my thoughts on this occasion—although, truthfully, I have forgotten that I still have birthdays to celebrate! In my memory, I have not had a birthday celebration such as this in well over twenty years!

As a child, I often pestered my parents about having birthday parties. They would say, "Children don't celebrate birthdays!" After I grew up and married, my husband showed his consideration for me by saying, "It is not worth it to have birthday parties! It is a nuisance to get presents and the celebration costs so much. All it does is remind you that you are getting older year after year. Since I love you and want to spare you this grief, I have decided not to remind you anymore of your accelerating years! Let's do away with any future birthday celebrations!"

In order to prove his good intentions, for twenty years he has not allowed us to suffer the nuisance of celebrating my birthday. As a result, we celebrate his birthday year after year to make sure that he remembers he is getting older, while he still cannot bear to let me have the opportunity to be reminded of my aging. So he is indeed a kind-hearted person. [audience laughter]

Perhaps it was due to this lack of awareness of birthday celebrations that I have been able to maintain a youthful attitude year after year and can never quite remember how old I am when a year has gone by. This continued until March 1989 when I gave birth to Engih and had a near death experience after the delivery. Ultimately my life was saved by Grand Master, who traveled out of his body to help me. I was reborn again. From that moment on, the significance of birthdays no longer pertained to the possession of this physical body. I no longer consider the date my mother gave birth to me as my only birthday. I asked myself these questions:

Which day is the day of true "birth?"

Since my arrival in the human world, which date is my "true birthday?"

I thought to myself, "The birthdays celebrated in the human world are not one's 'true birthdays!' One's true birthday is the day when one truly awakens to the essence of ones own nature." Only when one truly understands the nature of mind and realizes self-mastery is one truly "born."

To awaken this true "birthday," one needs teachings and guidance from an enlightened teacher of high wisdom. Therefore, I am aware that I am extremely fortunate to not have spent this life in vain because I have taken refuge in a realized Master—Living Buddha Lian-sheng Vajra Root Guru Sheng-yen Lu—who has reached Enlightenment through actual practice. Grand Master taught me that, apart from the physical body, one needs to gain a lucid understanding of the meaning of "true birth" and to seek eternal life. From that moment on, I knew I was no longer controlled by the numerals associated with the date on which my mother gave birth to me.

Now if someone asks me which day is my birthday, my reply is: I don't have a birthday. However, I also say: I do have a birthday, as every day is a day of rebirth for me and I live every single day in a state of mindfulness. As each day passes, life in this physical body is shortened, but I am ready to spontaneously leave the human realm at any moment. When one realizes that eternal life can never be bartered with anything in the material world, one's frame of mind naturally opens and grasps the truth that everything in the physical world is ultimately illusory. If one is still unable to tread on the path that leads to eternal life, then there is no difference between being physically alive or dead, and one is entrapped in this continuous cycle of coming and going.

Today you have given me a surprise birthday celebration and asked me to share with you my reflections on birthdays. How can I explain my feelings? In my heart, conventional birthdays no longer cause any stirrings or emotions. On the other hand, I do have a great depth of feeling regarding the subject. In a way, I now look at many things in a detached manner and can perceive them in both their positive and negative aspects. If one can transform the ego and its grasping of the physical world into the expansive and limitless Void, then there is nothing in the ordinary human world that can cause in one any tremendous emotion.

Again I would like to thank everyone for being so attentive in arranging this celebration. I just want to reiterate this: When one truly awakens to the essence of one's nature, understands the nature of the mind, and attains self-mastery, then one will arrive at one's true birthday. I sincerely wish for all of you attainment of a "true birthday."

Om Mani Padme Hum.

Chapter 5

Kuan Yin Ceremony in Houston

A talk by Master Samantha in Houston, Texas on July 30, 1995

(Q & A session with Grand Master)

His Holiness, fellow cultivators, ladies and gentlemen, good afternoon.

Om Mani Padme Hum.

First of all, I would like to express my gratitude to all the members of Mee Yee Tong (True Buddha Temple of Houston) for putting so much effort into the preparations for this ceremony. They have been working hard until two or three a.m. every day for the last several days, and that is why we have such a majestically decorated auditorium today for this Dharma Ceremony. Thank you very much. [audience applause]

We are also very grateful that our Root Guru, His Holiness Master Sheng-yen Lu, is paying his first visit to Houston. The students at Mee Yee Tong especially invited Grand Master to come to Houston to conduct a fire ceremony. Since it was not very suitable, due to various factors, to hold a large scale fire ceremony indoors, Mee Yee Tong students requested that Grand Master conduct, instead, a small scale fire ceremony, which took place yesterday evening at the local chapter, and I was asked to conduct today's public Kuan Yin Ceremony for Purification, Enhancement, Healing, and Bardo Deliverance. This has afforded me an opportunity to form an affinity with everyone here today. To me, this affinity truly seems like a wonderful opportunity that has fallen from the sky!

Prior to his arrival in Houston, the last stop of this itinerary, Grand Master visited five True Buddha School local chapters in the eastern states [in Chicago, Boston, New York, New Jersey, and North Carolina]. A dharma ceremony was held at each of those five stops, while here in Houston, Grand Master has bestowed his presence upon us at two ceremonies. This attests to the special karmic connection Mee Yee Tong has with Grand Master. [audience applause] While yesterday's fire ceremony was for students, today's dharma ceremony is for the public. Besides providing an opportunity for all the students here in Houston, Texas to develop their talents and potential, these two ceremonies also remind us that, as spiritual cultivators, we have to give consideration to people both inside and outside the school. In other words, we cannot just consider our own well being, but also, with a heart of equanimity, expand this well being to all others.

It has been almost nine and a half years since I took refuge in True Buddha School and embarked on the True Buddha Tantric practice. During these nine and a half years, my life has been extremely busy. Why? This was because, during the first four years, in addition to strengthening my own knowledge and being involved in affairs relating to the dharma, the local chapter, and the school, I was also busily involved in giving birth—I gave birth to three children in those four years! I was doing my own cultivation, propagating the True Buddha Tantric Dharma, and having children, all at the same time. Thinking back, I wonder how I managed to live through those four years.

During those years, when the children were still infants and toddlers, it was very difficult for me to totally abandon myself to the practice and propagation of the Dharma. It was a prolonged period of tempering of the self. I have often joked that, so far, there has not been another vajra master who has had to ring the bell and lead group cultivation with a baby strapped to her back. But that was the only way I could have done it! [audience laughter and applause]

I remember one time, after providing a consultation for a fellow student at the Purple Lotus Temple, the student suddenly became very anxious while I was energizing a Fu [talisman] for him. He asked, "Master Samantha, is my problem really very serious?"

I answered, "Not really! We will pray to the Buddhas and Bodhisattvas and to Grand Master, and the problem will be resolved."

"Then why is your energizing of the Fu so special this time?"

"What is it that is different?" I asked him.

"In the past, when you energized a Fu for me, only your hand would be moving. This time, I see that you are giving me a special energizing. I must be facing some extreme hardship that may not be easily resolved."

"I am not really doing anything different," I insisted.

He persisted, "You see, you used to use only your hand, but this time I noticed that your foot is also moving. Is my problem so serious that you are afraid to tell me?

I started to laugh and told him, "Come, come and take a look." I asked him to take a look under my desk.

After he took a look, he also started laughing. Why? Under the desk my three children were taking a nap. One of them was fidgeting and about to wake up. In order to keep him asleep, I was gently patting his bottom, rocking him back to sleep. If he woke up, I would have had to fix him a bottle of milk. Next to my feet, the three children had curled up like three little kittens.

Having to face such hardships during that period has strengthened me and taught me a great deal. To cultivate is to attain a pure heart and to overcome various kinds of habitual tendencies. If one simultaneously must seriously cope with secular affairs, obstacles are often very difficult to overcome. But if one is seriously devoted to spiritual practice, one will have a kind of spiritual support that helps one to pull through such an experience. At the time, I did not have the financial means to hire a baby sitter, so I had to take care of the children myself. Even so, I never wavered in my practice of the True Buddha Tantric Dharma.

I remember that, during those days, when I entered into deep meditation in front of the shrine, the children would be crawling around me, sometimes all over me, grabbing my hair, playing with the bell, or even using the vajra to knock on my head. I still continued to do my practice! [audience laughter] Sometimes I entered

73

so deeply into samadhi that I did not come out, even when the children had climbed on me and pulled my head to the floor. Thinking back, that kind of environment was indeed very interesting and difficult, but I have persisted in my spiritual practice. In fact, those difficult times have better equipped me to walk the present and future stages of my path.

During the last several years, as the children were growing a little older, I have been acting on the orders of Grand Master to start teaching the dharma in other parts of the world. Since the birth of my youngest son six and a half years ago, I have started traveling. My count is that I have visited local chapters of the True Buddha School in 21 countries. I sometimes think, how have I managed to walk such a path?

For example, on April 30th, we left San Francisco to attend a dharma ceremony in Taiwan conducted by Grand Master. We did not return to the United States until July 21st. During a period of almost three months, every day was spent in the same way as the last several days I have spent here at Mee Yee Tong—busy from morning till night, without any break. This is because every local chapter has had many things that needed to be taken care of. During this time, I spent thirty-three days in Malaysia. After deducting two days of flight time, I had been left thirty-one days to visit thirty local chapters. In fact, as I had to stop over again on the return trip at several of the local chapters to conduct dharma ceremonies, I had actually visited a total of thirty-six local chapters in thirty-one days. It was a very hectic schedule filled with dharma ceremonies, consultations, teaching, consecration, and purification of shrines. Such a very busy schedule can only be endured by someone with good physical health, spiritual support, and a strong blessing from our Root Guru.

Three of our reverends had accompanied me on this trip and they asked me if Grand Master had taught me any special practice to enable me to have such vigorous energy and speak so loudly when I was only averaging two to three hours of sleep each night. I truthfully told them that the most important factor behind my energy is my spiritual support.

Where does this spiritual support come from? My spiritual support comes from knowing exactly "what I am doing." I am clearly aware of my life task and why I am carrying it out. When one sees this more clearly than the other people around one, one's heart will be moved and energy will be generated, urging one to continuously forge ahead.

Ever since I started on this journey to propagate the dharma, I have cherished every single day. I also consider that each encounter with each country, stop over, or person could be my last. This is because six and a half years ago, in 1989, I suffered a post-partum hemorrhage and underwent a near death experience. I only came back to this life because of our Guru's intervention. Ever since that moment, my heart has undergone a great transformation. I deeply feel the impermanence of human life. You may be alive and well and own everything one moment, but your condition can be completely altered and everything will be lost in the next second. When you realize that all the mundane things you have been working so hard to amass do not ultimately belong to you, what will your outlook be?

I have deeply felt what it is like to be living in the last moment. Therefore, after my return to this world, my state of mind was completely altered. This realization of impermanence has stayed with me ever since. The present condition or human state, be it good or bad, can very possibly disperse in a flash and never reassemble. It is somehow regretful that the same personalities will never be gathered together again, but no man is eternal. That is why I cherish every person who passes by, regardless of the condition he or she is in. After all, we may never meet again. So how can I not try to seize the moment?

If a negative karmic connection exists between a certain individual and myself, and this karmic enmity cannot be resolved right away, I then try to open my heart. One of the methods taught to us by Grand Master is to visualize the faces of people whom one dislikes and with whom one cannot get along, and to transform their faces into our own face. One may hold grudges against others (disputes between human beings often originate in self-grasping) and one may dislike and find fault with others, but one seldom dislikes, blames, or scolds oneself.

Therefore, I often visualize other people's faces transforming into my own face. After doing this for a while, I began to discover that people's faces are my own, and that every person seems to turn into me. When every person is really me, what is there for me to get upset or fight about?

The most important point is that the True Buddha Tantric Dharma, taught to us by Grand Master, helps us to expand our consciousness and experience positive transformations. This is done by visualizing the merging of the Buddhas or Bodhisattvas into our heart. When one becomes unified with the Buddhas or Bodhisattvas, an infinite expansion of one's heart can occur.

I remember a long time ago, soon after I took refuge, I went to see Grand Master. I asked him, "Is there any special Tantric practice to help one eliminate the three poisons of greed, hatred, and ignorance?" This question arose because I had seen some esoteric books listing mudras and mantras for eradicating the three poisons. It occurred to me that, in our True Buddha School, there might also exist some special, speedy practice to completely dissolve one's greed, hatred, and ignorance. I wanted a short-cut method.

All I got from Grand Master was a curt reply, "Do your [True Buddha Tantric Dharma] practice." I remember thinking to myself, "Of course I know that, but what I want is some special short-cut method." I repeated the question and, again, all I got was the same reply, "Do your practice." I had flown to Seattle especially to ask this question, and all I received was that curt answer.

Do not look down on this simple answer. Those words from Grand Master, although seemingly very casual, are words of empowerment. After all my planning, after spending money and time for the trip, I received only those few words, "Do your practice." So I returned to the Purple Lotus Temple in San Francisco.

I imprinted his words "do your practice" on my heart. How can one eradicate the three poisons? By doing an honest practice. If one does not plant one's feet on such solid ground and seriously start doing the practice, step by step, to transform all of one's non-virtuous actions, speeches, and thoughts, one will continue to experience both physical and emotional disturbances. All supplications are in vain if one does not put in an honest effort to do the actual practice to effect transformations. As shown by the True Buddha Tantric Dharma, efficacy is demonstrated when one actually does the practices and not merely talks about it.

Yesterday, Mee Yee Tong took us to see the Ringling Brothers' Circus in town, and we had a chance to enjoy all those remarkable acts performed by the skillful circus artists. The physical condition and skills displayed by the artists demonstrate long years of training. Their acts require such precision in timing and co-ordination that any slight negligence can result in very obvious failures. One also gets the feeling that these artists must engage in a very persistent routine of training. It is the same with spiritual practice. If one does not engage in daily practice, to vigorously remind and correct oneself, then one will not be able to judge the situation presented in a spiritually correct and objective manner.

I really admire the circus performers I saw yesterday. For our enjoyment and understanding they presented their best acts, a result of hard work and training. They made us feel that there was no need for language. During the performance of the trapeze act, for example, no special words were needed to explain what was going to happen next, as everything is actually demonstrated in front of everyone. No matter which city or country they are from, they give us their best performance. Watching, I could not help but feel the superfluity of language.

As long as one has trained regularly and is well prepared, one may let the audience be the judge during the real show. If the show is good, people will applaud; if the show is bad, people will sigh. Any accompanying commentary only serves as hype; what makes or breaks a show still depends on true skill and artistry.

Similarly, actions, rather than words, reveal more about the spiritual maturity of a practitioner. One may be able to expound on great doctrines, but can one actualize them? One may be telling others to open up the heart but, when the moment of challenge arrives, can one really let go of the ego? Or does one continue to voice one's grievances and try to argue and justify one's actions through all kinds of channels? How one reacts is dependent on one's spiritual maturity and understanding.

I admire very much the words spoken by the Sixth Patriarch Hui-neng to his teacher, as shown in the following story. On one occasion, Hui-neng and his teacher were going to cross a river. As the teacher was about to pick up the paddle, Hui-neng grabbed the paddle and said, "Master, allow me. When one is lost, one relies on the teacher; when one is awakened, one relies on oneself." I gasped in admiration when I first came upon these words, and they have stayed with me ever since.

The Sixth Patriarch spent only a very short time in the presence of his teacher. In the middle of the night, his teacher transmitted to him a few brief words of heart-teachings, and Hui-neng immediately attained conceptual realization. However, conceptual realization is one thing, actualization of this realization is another matter! After attaining conceptual realization, the next step is to practice, act, and integrate this into one's life. Therefore, the Sixth Patriarch made this remark to his teacher, "When I was lost and deluded, you taught and enlightened me. Now that I understand the essence of this practice to reach liberation, you need not help me anymore, for I must walk on my own to reach the goal."

I have often spurred myself forward with those words from the Sixth Patriarch. In fact, the number of liberation gateways our Guru has taught us has far exceeded what was transmitted from the Fifth to the Sixth Patriarch. By engaging in any one of the True

Buddha Tantric Dharma practices, one will be able to attain a swift realization, just as the Sixth Patriarch did. Through his hard labor, our Guru has produced for us volumes of written and spoken works. If one will only pay careful attention to these words, receiving into one's heart even one single sentence, one will be able to tune into our Guru's heart and spirit. After realization, continue to actualization—words and ideas not backed by action have no substance.

While on the path of actualization, regard all adversities, great or small, as necessary for one's experience and learning. As one overcomes each of these hurdles, a deep gratitude will well up inside one. Why? Without these trials and tribulations, one would not be able to reach a higher level of realization. Through human interaction and the managing of human affairs, one learns tolerance, acceptance, forgiveness, and how to better get along with others. When one encounters the repeat of a difficult situation, one will no longer be perplexed or agitated. One will know how to handle the matter at hand because one has already experienced it. Each challenge is a learning process and, through problem solving, wisdom is generated.

Since I do not have many opportunities to go to Seattle to be with our Guru and learn from him, I cherish every one of my meetings with him. On one occasion, I went to ask him this specific question, "How should I do my practice in order to become as whole and perfect as you?" When I look at our Guru, I am awed by his majestic wholeness and the manifestation of the thirty-two marks of Buddhahood. He gave me this reply, "I am Amitabha, and Amitabha is me."

Upon hearing this declaration, an ordinary person who has not entered into a certain state of mind might find our Guru to be very arrogant. He or she might react, "Oh! A man is just a man! How can one regard oneself as Amitabha?" Such a reaction indicates lack of wisdom and a contracted state of mind. However, to me at that one moment, Guru's words went straight to my heart. From that day on, I have been repeating to myself over and over again, "I am Amitabha, and Amitabha is me." It is the same as when Shakyamuni Buddha was born. While pointing one hand to the sky and the other to earth, he uttered, "Between heaven and earth, only I am the highest." People who fail to understand the true meaning of the "I" denounce him for being preposterous and arrogant.

After hearing this reply from our Guru, "I am Amitabha," I went home and started contemplating on its inherent meaning. Kuan Yin is my Personal Deity in this lifetime. Therefore, after obtaining a very majestic picture of her, I have been imprinting her image in my mind every day and invoking her to enter my heart to unite with me. Throughout my daily activities, I try my best to visualize myself as Kuan Yin and Kuan Yin as me. When I am at the verge of losing my temper, I immediately remind myself that I am Kuan Yin. How can I then lose my temper and commit a wrong speech?

If my children misbehave, and I am provoked to raise my hand on them, the inner voice will speak, "I am Kuan Yin," and my raised hand will be lowered.

Ever since, I have been using this method of "merging with the Personal Deity" to spur myself and reform my habitual and improper words and behaviors. Then one day the mystical and inexplicable happened: I actually found myself transformed into Kuan Yin. It was an expansive and completely boundless experience. My state of mind was completely transformed and all aspects of myself, even including the way I walked, became new and different. I was ecstatic because I finally understood our Guru's words, "I am Amitabha, and Amitabha is me."

I have only one possible regret from this whole transformation: perhaps the picture that I secured for visualization is a chubby Kuan Yin and, by constant visualizing myself as her, I have also become very chubby! [audience laughter] Next time I have to find a picture of a more slender Kuan Yin. Or, I should focus on my heart being expanded without the stomach following suit. An enlarged stomach holds more food and has contributed to my overweight status. What happens is that, with the relaxation of the heart, one tends to gain more weight.

Self-cultivation through practicing the True Buddha Tantric Dharma has brought me countless spiritual responses, the most crucial being the kind of transformation about which I just spoke.

Earlier, as I was registering for the ceremony, I heard this conversation among some students. One of them asked, "How much of an offering should I make when I go up to receive empowerment from Grand Master?" Another replied, "Grand Master has said that it is completely up to each individual." "Well, what is the minimum then?" "It is all as you wish. If you want to give a lot, then give a lot; if you want to give a little, then give a little." A third student then offered this opinion, "That means if you want to give one dollar, then give one dollar; if you want to give five or ten dollars, then give five or ten dollars. It is up to you completely."

Perhaps the person who was wondering how much of an offering to make was a newcomer and really had no idea at all. Someone next to him made this suggestion, "Just go with the lower price. [audience laughter] After all, who can tell how much of an offering is inside the red envelope? It makes no difference whether it is one or one hundred dollars, does it?" Hearing this conversation brought up a lot of feelings in me. In the beginning, soon after taking refuge, I also had no idea how much of an offering was appropriate for an empowerment. There was often this suggestion, "Just give one or two dollars; it is all as you wish anyway." Since I was new and did not know much, I picked up on that idea and only gave one or two dollars. As there was no set fee, I would pull out the lowest denomination from my wallet. This kind of consideration has probably occurred to everyone.

However, the longer I do spiritual cultivation and the further along the path I walk, the more I am able to understand the teaching of our Guru, and the more I realize why our Guru has said that the amount of an offering is completely up to us. Only a master of the highest realization would tell us this: make the offering as you wish. As a Buddhist practitioner, do you know what is it that you wish for in doing the practice? What is the meaning of cultivating the Buddhadharma? After taking refuge in the True Buddha School, what is your goal in practicing the True Buddha Tantric Dharma? One has to know the answers to these questions.

"As you wish...," What is that you wish? In practicing the True Buddha Tantric Dharma, if you do not know what you are wishing for, and if you do not know how to express your appreciation for the Guru, Buddhas, and Dharma, you will probably give the "cheapest" offering.

I have in the past participated in Dharma Ceremonies given by other schools. To attend a lecture or receive an empowerment from the rinpoches or Dharma masters, one must pay a certain fixed fee. For example, twenty dollars for an empowerment or ten dollars for attending a ceremony. Under such circumstances, when everyone is paying the same price, one actually feels restricted by the fixed price and is reluctant to make a bigger offering to express one's gratitude for the teaching.

However, if one really understands the true meaning of "as you wish," and the true efficacy of the invisible transformative power of the empowerments (to remove potential disasters and enhance one's fortunes and wisdom), one realizes that a few dollars in offering is not really enough. If one cherishes the Dharma and appreciates the Guru's compassionately motivated desire to help one attain Enlightenment, one would not be inspired to make the "cheapest" offering.

I have previously given the example of a fellow student who only makes offerings when he has special supplications and, after donating a little of his effort, he makes sure that everyone knows about it. Too often one keeps tab on the few charitable acts one does, and fails to keep count of the many transgressions one commits from morning till night. When one fails to see transgressions as transgressions, one continues to commit them. When one regards charity as only benefiting others and not oneself, one refrains from doing charitable acts.

I remember our Guru has taught us, "A practitioner should engage in tasks that benefit both the self and others, and refrain from tasks that benefit only the self and not others. However, if an action benefits others and not the self, one must still do it."

I have used this teaching as a yardstick. If a task is only advantageous to me and does not benefit anyone else, why should I do it? If such a task only enhances my chance of creating negative karma for myself, why should I carry it out? Therefore, I often question my own motives before doing something and use these teachings as guidelines. From this approach, I have learned a great deal.

Put your best effort into the learning and practice of the True Buddha Tantric Dharma. Our Guru has written over one hundred books. When you truly understand the content and spirit of these books, you will have a new outlook on life and be able to embrace it whole-heartedly. This is what I have experienced.

I am also extremely grateful to our Guru for transmitting to us such great esoteric practices, in particular the fire ceremony which we had yesterday. He has said that a Tantric practitioner can achieve great accomplishment through the following three practices: mantra recitation, Samadhi, and fire puja. I myself have received great inner guidance, this-worldly and other-worldly, through the practice of fire offerings. Whenever I wholeheartedly carry out a fire offering, I always receive great response. Although many other supplications that we make do not manifest right away, what is most important is that, during the fire offering, one may in a flash let go of the "self" and become one with the Universal Self. It is a reward so infinite that no secular benefit can compare with it. It brings great bliss characterized by clarity and brightness.

Regarding worldly supplications, I try my best and then leave the arrangements and results up to the Divine. This way I am able to walk my path in a natural and carefree manner. I am very grateful that I have been

87

provided with all these experiences, to learn and use what I have experienced to help numerous fellow students and other sentient beings overcome their confusion and delusions.

The benefits of cultivating the True Buddha Tantric Dharma are, indeed, countless. Responses attained in the inner being cannot be described in words; only by engaging in the practice oneself may one directly experience them.

All of us present here today are fortunate because our Guru entered into samadhi earlier during the Dharma Ceremony to give us blessings. I have here many questions that have been submitted by the members of the audience. Because of time constraints, I have looked over the questions and picked out the ones that are the most representative. We invite Grand Master to answer these questions for us and to give guidance on how we can, through the practice of the True Buddha Tantric Dharma, speedily eliminate all obscurations that have been accumulated in this life and our past lives, and to quickly attain special accomplishments. Thank you, everyone. Om Mani Padme Hum.

Question and Answer Session at the True Buddha Dharma Ceremony in Houston, Texas on July 30, 1995.

[Q]   [Master Samantha] Here, on behalf of everyone, I will ask our Root Guru to give us guidance. Please give our Root Guru a great welcome with your warmest applause. (audience applause) I have a question submitted by an audience member who is probably not a True Buddha student. He has written here: Living Buddha Lian-sheng, what are the differences between exoteric and esoteric Buddhism? What are the differences between the True Buddha School and other esoteric Buddhist schools? Please compassionately instruct us.

[A]   [Grand Master] **It is like this. Exoteric Buddhism was taught by Shakyamuni Buddha, and it consists of theories that can be understood or perceived on an external or apparent level. Esoteric Buddhism, on the other hand, was transmitted by Vairocana Buddha, the Great Sun Buddha. Most of the teachings of Esoteric Buddhism deal with the achievement of inner realization, through practical methods that are more secretive, or involved with one's inner being. This is the greatest difference between the exoteric and esoteric schools in Buddhism. Remember, if someone asks you in the future, "What is an exoteric school?" An exoteric school teaches apparent doctrines. "What is an esoteric school?" An esoteric school teaches the secrets of inner realization. This is a topic to which one may devote a great deal of time, but it all boils down to this one main difference.**

What then are the differences between the True Buddha School and the other esoteric Buddhist schools? Actually, I have received lineage transmission from the other esoteric Buddhist schools. In the Kagyu School, my guru is the Sixteenth Karmapa; in the Sakya School; my guru is Master Sakya Cheng Kung; in the Nyingma School, my guru is Revered Liao Ming; and in the Gelugpa, my guru is Guru Thubten Taerchi.

However, I have found the existing esoteric practices to be loaded with trivial details. Therefore, I have tossed out the dross, selected the essentials, and formulated them into the True Buddha Liturgy. Mee Yee Tong is named after Mee Yee which means the esoteric liturgy of the True Buddha School or True Buddha Tantric Dharma. By formulating it and engaging in its actual practice, I recognize the True Buddha Tantric Dharma to be the quintessence of all esoteric practices. This is the major difference between the True Buddha School and other esoteric Buddhist schools. One other slight difference is that I have confirmed for True Buddha School practitioners the establishment of a Siddhi or Pure Land which differs from the Pure Lands of the other esoteric schools. That is all. Thank you. [audience applause]

[Q] The second question is: The goal of cultivation is to reach Enlightenment and attain Buddhahood. But this is such a difficult goal to attain. Besides, even if one arrives at the goal, one has to come back to the human world to help other sentient beings and therefore one risks becoming deluded and contaminated again. In that case, what is the point of doing spiritual cultivation?

[A]   **This is a very good question. I have had a student tell me, "I don't want to become a Buddha." So I asked her, "What do you want to become then?" She replied, "I want to be a dog in the United States."** [audience laughter] **She feels that dogs in America, being pets, are well fed and taken care of by their owners. She would rather be a dog than a Buddha. This question reflects a similar sentiment as expressed by that student. Why? If one becomes a Buddha and has to reincarnate in order to fulfill one's vow of helping sentient beings, it is indeed a hardship!**

Let us take Master Samantha as an example. Earlier in her speech, she told us how she had to do cultivation, be with her three small children, and travel to many countries --- a very hectic and tiring job! Why make oneself so tired? Actually, when she was talking about the circus performers, my feeling was to be glad that I wasn't one of those trapeze artists! [audience laughter] **If I were one of them, I would worry every day about the risks involved. Of course we gasp in admiration when we watch them perform, but I don't wish to be one of them. Who would want to be one of them? It is a lot of hard work**

and very tiring. But attaining Buddhahood is not the same. Throughout the entire process of cultivation, I have experienced no regrets. I have no emotional afflictions now, only liberation and freedom.

Besides, it was Master Samantha and not I who had to give birth to all those children. [audience laughter] Of course, I can still procreate after attaining Buddhahood. I have the ability and the strength and the power to procreate, but I choose not to. I can have my own way and enter into the state of limitless transformation and manifestation. This is the advantage of attaining Buddhahood. When I feel like entering into Nirvana, I enter into Nirvana. When I feel like coming back to this world to teach, I come back again. This is known as the state of spontaneous transformation and manifestation—a very high realm of Buddhahood.

Buddhists know that "releasing of the self" and "attaining sovereignty" refer to this state of spontaneous transformation and manifestation. It is a very transcendental realm. In this realm, one may use one's "thoughts" to effect transformation and manifestation. Isn't it a very wonderful state? There is no misery at all. I am very happy.

That is why I had to save Master Samantha's life. Now she runs around and does these things so that I can be free! [audience laughter and applause] She told us how hectic her schedule was and how hard she had to struggle with cultivation, helping others, and taking care of her three children, but, earlier during this Dharma Ceremony, I was sitting here and almost fell asleep. [uproar of audience laughter] **This is the benefit of attaining Buddhahood.** [audience laughter] **You can delegate your responsibilities to your students. Why do you have to do them yourself? Right?**

Just now, the director of Mee Yee Tong, Lianhua Chien-sheng, offered me a big bundle of red envelopes and a white silk scarf. It seems that Master Samantha was not offered anything, right? [audience laughter] **He did not offer the silk scarf to her, just to me. But it was she who did all the work,** [audience laughter] **and not I! I took the red envelopes and my pocket is full. I really feel happy!** [audience uproar] **Master Samantha had to work so hard, give a long speech, and during the ceremony, she had to perform the dance of mudras and to chant with everyone. Really, when you were all reciting the Universal Gate Chapter of the Lotus Sutra, I was trying very hard to fight off the sandman.** [audience uproar] **I almost gave in to him. But, as I was sitting on the highest spot in this auditorium, how could I justify falling asleep?**

Sometimes when that happens, I just explain to students that I am communicating with the Buddas and Bodhisattvas. [audience laughter] **Actually I could not keep my head from nodding! I enjoy a lot of leisure now, while Master Samantha has become very anxious. She had to hold meetings with the members** of the Mee Yee Tong to discuss the organizing of this ceremony, sacrificing her rest and sleep. I told her, "Relax, it really doesn't matter!" [audience laughter] The arising of causes and conditions is followed by the extinction of causes and conditions. After the disintegration of a certain cause and condition, another will arise.

The question asked by this student is: If, after attaining Buddhahood, one has to come back to help other beings and work so hard, why bother to do cultivation at all? One asks this question because one does not know that, after attaining Buddhahood, one will have freedom and leisure! [audience laughter and applause] **Bodhisattvas** who have not reached Buddhahood are quite miserable and have to work till they drop! They have to perform mudras, maneuver the vajra and bell, and supplicate blessings for everyone! I just sit here with nothing to do! [audience laughter]

After attaining sovereignty, one may be as free or as busy as one likes. It is completely up to the individual. One abides in a state of ecstasy, the result of practicing the Vajrayana method of "union of bliss and emptiness." I have the ability to procreate, but I choose not to. I assure you that this is not an ordinary but an extraordinary ability. Having an ordinary ability is useless. To practice Vajrayana is to acquire extraordinary energy, strength, non-outflow, and non-birth. When you acquire these, you too will be

free and sovereign. You will not have any household burdens and you will be eternally happy. From the state of liberation and freedom, it is quite amusing to watch the dramas of the sentient beings unfolding and changing.

Such are the benefits of attaining Buddhahood. All of these several masters sitting below me have to work, [audience laughter] **while I just sit leisurely and watch. It is very nice.** [audience applause]

[Q]   The third question is: Grand Master, is there any method to help one to develop tolerance and endurance? Is there any special Tantric practice to help one to be more cheerful and not be dispirited by problems caused by human interaction?

[A]   **In a way, Master Samantha has already addressed this problem in her speech. She has offered a very good approach—when one sees others as oneself, one will not try to bully oneself. Right? When one stops bullying oneself, one learns tolerance. So first start with oneself.**

There is another approach. In this world, almost every person is afflicted with narcissism and loves his or her self the most. This is the basis for all self-interest. I am just the opposite, I dislike myself the most. If one learns to regard oneself as the lowest and

everyone else as higher, then one will learn tolerance and endurance. So, when people criticize you, turn that into a learning experience.

You have seen me criticizing a certain Buddhist master. I do not criticize casually. I took the time and painstakingly read all of his written work before I evaluated him. I feel that he has many enviable qualities which I don't have, but I want him to be better. Therefore, I pointed out a slight blemish of his to spur him on. If he accepts my criticism, he can become a perfect Buddha.

I myself have many shortcomings, and I am always learning. With this in mind, I learn endurance and tolerance. Since I dislike myself and am always learning from other people's strengths, I welcome any criticism of me. This is how I would answer this question. [audience applause]

[Q]   Grand Master, what does the Vajrayana term "Buddhahood in the Present Body" mean?

[A]   There is great learning behind this term. In Vajrayana, the term refers to the attainment of instantaneous Buddhahood in the present body, without going through the bardo state, or reliance on a spiritual guide in the bardo state.

Buddhahood through the bardo state takes place when one is unable to attain Buddhahood while alive. After one dies, one's spirit leaves the body, enters into the bardo state, and meets with Amitabha who leads one to Sukhavati. In Sukhavati, one continues to study, to become educated, until one attains the qualifications to become a Buddha. This is Buddhahood through the bardo state.

To achieve Buddhahood in the Present Body, one studies and practices in this world what one would have to study in Sukhavati. The method taught in Sukhavati to attain Buddhahood is, instead, practiced here. Having taken this tutorial class, one may directly ascend to the realm of Buddhahood. Even though Amitabha, Kuan Yin, and Mahasthamaprata do not come to give one guidance, one knows the way. This is Buddhahood in the Present Body. If Amitabha, Kuan Yin, and Mahasthamaprata come to guide one to Sukhavati, it is definitely a case of Buddhahood through the bardo state.

When one abides in the Buddha Nature, one may immediately travel to Sukhavati and arrive at the highest realm, the Realm of Eternal Tranquility and Light. This is Buddhahood in the Present Body. In Vajrayana, Buddhahood in the Present Body is attained through the practices of Highest Tantra Yoga and Great Perfection, which enable one to abide directly in the radiant nature of the mind. Thank you.

[audience applause]

[Q]   Grand Master, when I first started doing Buddhist cultivation, I had very good intentions and was very sincere and devout. But why has my temper been getting worse and my voice getting louder? After each incidence of losing my temper, I realize my mistake and feel remorse. However, when the situation repeats itself, I again become deluded and hold fast to my own opinion. I fly into a rage and clash with the other party. Why has this happened? [audience laughter]

[A]   **This is human nature. Almost without exception, men are like this. That is why, it is said, a Buddhist will absolutely attain Buddhahood if he or she can maintain the original aspiration. Shakyamuni Buddha stated that if one does not falter from the original aspiration, one will definitely become a Buddha.**

Most people are very determined when they initially aspire to do the practice. But, due to lack of perseverance, they gradually wander from the path. In a way, this is analogous to chewing a piece of gum. In the beginning, the flavor of the chewing gum is great but, the longer one chews, the less taste remains. Finally, the gum becomes totally flat and, in the end, one spits it out! [audience laughter]

Spiritual cultivation is similar. Initially, one finds the experience exhilarating but, in the end, it becomes like a chewed-up piece of gum and one loses the determination to go on. It is the same with

chewing on a stick of sugar cane. After the sugar cane has been chewed for a while, it loses its sweetness and is spit out. This is human nature.

It is almost the same with marriage. That is why marriage is described as the tomb of love. In the beginning, everything is fresh and exciting; then, later on, it becomes as bland as a glass of water. Does Coca Cola or water have more taste to it? Of course, there are cases when people are able to find deep and satisfying experiences in quietude. In these cases spiritual cultivation will be a success.

Today we know that spiritual cultivation is the greatest aspiration one can have as a human being. Besides offering a meaning to life, it has extraordinary intrinsic value. It is therefore very important to persevere in the original goal and to constantly fortify it.

How does one fortify one's initial aspiration? Let me tell you, in the practice of Tantrayana, when one succeeds in practices associated with the first level, second level, or third level of empowerment, there is a real development of spiritual power within one. This power will enable one to more easily persevere in one's original determination.

I have seen many senior spiritual practitioners. After engaging for a very long time in the practice of chanting, they still come to ask me if they can be reborn to Sukhavati. This shows that they have not yet had any vision of the Buddha, or any glimpse into the nature of the mind. If one has received some kind of spiritual response, one's original aspiration will be fortified. During the course of one's cultivation, episode after episode of spiritual experience will occur to strengthen one's will and determination to continue on the path.

For myself, each higher level I reached was confirmed by a certain expansion of consciousness and perception. I can see the descending of the light from the Buddhas and Bodhisattvas and perceive their movements. Indeed, I can read my own destiny. When you are able to experience such validations, your original aspiration will persevere and become very strong, and you will not recede from the path. Spiritual responses play a very significant role in the practice of Vajrayana. When one starts to experience the spiritual responses in Vajrayana, and when these experiences continue to occur, one is able to fortify one's original aspiration and to develop perseverance. Otherwise, it is hard to avoid deviating from the path. [audience applause]

[Q] Grand Master, please explain the various experiences associated with samadhi. For example, how can I differentiate the experiences of earth, water, fire, wind, and space? This is to provide a kind of reference so that I will not become afraid or perplexed during samadhi.

[A]   The person who asks this question must have done some study in this area or already had some solid experiences of samadhi. The Buddha himself taught many methods for entering into samadhi. The major or minor "chih and kuan" [alternating cessation of thought with visualization], breath counting, and the Vajrayana method of viewing emptiness can all help one to enter into samadhi.

But I feel that a very good method to achieve mental cessation is still the Vajrayana visualization method. This involves three steps. First of all, one visualizes the purest moon appearing. Next, one visualizes the manifestation of a seed syllable from which the Personal Deity emerges. Third, one proceeds to do the visualization of merging the Personal deity and oneself: the entering of the Personal Deity into one's body and the entering of the self into the Personal Deity. In Vajrayana this is known as the "three steps of engendering": moon disc, seed syllable, and Personal Deity. If one repeatedly practices this visualization, the distance between you and the Personal Deity will be shortened and there will be a mutual convergence of the self and the Personal Deity—a very important accomplishment.

Earlier, Master Samantha talked about how she visualized herself as Kuan Yin and how I told her that I was Amitabha. In Vajrayana this technique is known as "self-ennobling." The Buddhas are proud of their state of being, while a human being is proud of his or her state of being. In Vajrayana or esoteric schools, there exist practices to transform this self-pride into Buddhaic pride. Exoteric schools dismiss this type of visualization as being too "egotistical." Actually, a continuous visualization of oneself as a Buddha can, indeed, result in the visualization becoming a reality. This type of "self-ennobling" is a kind of "chih kuan" method. A "chih kuan" method employs visualization [kuan] to stop [chih] all other thoughts. Variations of the "chih kuan" method are found in both exoteric and esoteric schools.

Thus, with prolonged practice of this "chih kuan" method, there will eventually come the moment when one is able to bring all mental energy into one point. When this happens, the internal fire will be lit. This internal fire may be used to heat the essences inside one's subtle energy body and transform them into crystallized light drops. This first involves the interaction between the elements of fire and water and, subsequently, the transformation of water into earth. The crystallized light drops are earth. After this, the raising or elevation of the crystallized light drops results in wind. When the light drops further transform into bright luminosity, it results in space. These are the transformations in the subtle energy level.

Fire heats water, water turns into earth, earth becomes wind, and wind enters into space. This is the

procedure for the above transformations. Thank you.
[audience applause]

[Q]   Grand Master, at night, when I sleep, I often experience being weighed down by ghosts. I have done "armor protection," "sacred boundary setting," "sleeping maha-mudra," and "vajra visualization" all to no avail. What should I do? Is there a more powerful method that you can teach me?

[A]   **There is another method I can teach you. What is it? When you are being weighed down by a ghost, just let it be!** [audience laughter] **Let me tell you, do not be afraid! People become so afraid and nervous at bedtime when they have such encounters, but the ghosts cannot kill you. Has anyone died from being weighed down by a ghost? You are still around to ask this question, aren't you?** [audience laughter]

In my case, ghosts don't weigh me down. It is the other way around, I put my weight on them. [audience laughter] **Every time the ghosts see me, they start to shiver. During my frequent teaching trips, I have to stay in hotels, and I practice my vajra fists exercise at night, instead of in the morning, to evict all these ghosts from my room.**

Therefore, I bully the ghosts instead of the other way around. To be a Tantric practitioner is to have power over the ghosts and not be bullied by them. Make no mistake on that. Your chi has to be so

strong and powerful that ghosts run away from you when they see you. How can you let them weigh you down? To let this happen is already to be lost. You have to sit on them. That is why every time I am in a hotel and see ghosts, they will start to scream and yell as I chase after them. [audience laugher] **Then, after evicting them, I have my room sealed so that I may have a restful sleep.**

First of all, you must exercise to develop a "vajra energy body" and a very strong and powerful chi. When you step inside a room, sweep your eyes around the room to reveal all the ghosts inside. In my next book, which is soon to be published, *The Magic of Tantrayana*, I have devoted a chapter to special ghostbusting methods. [audience laughter]

[Q]   Grand Master, whenever I see monks and nuns, I admire their spirit of renunciation to seek the Tao and liberation, I also know that the ritual of ordination is very simple, that one only needs to submit a request and then submit to a tonsure ceremony. But what happens if one's disposition remains the same before and after one's head is shorn? What if one's disposition gets worse? Can one return to a householder's life? Doesn't one create negative karma by putting on a monk's robe only externally?

[A]   **It is like this. The inherent meaning of the vow of ordination is to make a commitment to seek** liberation. It is very good that you have this desire to make a commitment because, in this world, everything eventually returns to emptiness. A successful career, a fulfilling marriage, or a high position will ultimately transform into emptiness. Spouse, money, children, and position will become emptiness in the future. Only the path of spiritual cultivation has a transcendental value.

It is very good that you have generated the bodhicitta to take the renunciation vow. I also advocate the vow of renunciation, but I will not force anyone who is not ready. Why? One may still have many unfinished karmic loose ends in the world. Such unfinished business and mundane affinities have to be brought to a close before one may become a monk or nun. It is very good if one can take the ordination vow. If one cannot, this is also fine, as one must first finish one's business with the world.

But what happens if, after ordination, one still cannot change one's nature? Do not worry about this now. When you get to that stage, I will teach you! [audience laughter] You worry too much, don't you? You have not even taken the vow yet! Why worry about something that has not even happened? [audience uproar and applause]

The truth is, do not worry too soon. We Taiwanese have a saying, "Shoulder the load when you have to; make a pot of yam soup if you run out of rice."

[Q]   Grand Master, why do some people have such an easy time making money, while others have it so hard? I have been doing the Jambhala practice for a very long time, but I still have not made any extra money. Have I made some kind of transgression? [audience laughter]

[A]   **It is true that some people make money easily while others do not. For example, there are people who invest in foreign currencies and make a lot of money. Since the rate of exchange of foreign currencies fluctuates, by knowing which foreign currency is rising, one can make money by converting one's assets to that country's currency. By this type of transaction, a great deal of money can be made. Investors may have millions of U.S. dollars in their accounts, and this money may grow many times, just by this kind of maneuvering. Such money can grow even though the investors are not doing much in the way of hard work. On the other hand, some people work very hard and earn very little money, even by working two jobs.**

Why has there been no spiritual response from the Jambhala even after one has done the Jambhala Practice for a very long time? This is because one has not accumulated enough merits.

To receive enhancement through the practice of the Buddhadharma, one must first remove one's obscurations. That is why the Vajrayana white purification yoga is listed ahead of the other karma

yogas [of enhancement, magnetization, and subjugation]. First, do the purification and repentance practices to amass your merits. When your merits have reached a certain point, the Jambhala will bestow blessings upon you. Although you have been doing the Jambhala practice, do keep in mind that, even if you manage to gain some money, disasters will follow if you are not backed up by merits.

Last night I talked about how each person has his or her own fate. Yet Buddhism does not advocate fate because the practice of Buddhism can change the hold of fate on men. By practicing the repentance yoga, purification yoga, and the Jambhala yoga, one can change one's fate and increase one's merits. That was why **Yuan Liao Fan** [the author of *Four Essays on Karma*] devoted himself to a life of charity, so as to alter his predestined course. By practicing generosity and charity, one will enhance one's blessings. By doing Buddhadharma cultivation today, one shall increase one's blessings, as well as wisdom.

Therefore, do not indulge in any vain hopes of receiving fortunes from the Jambhala before the removal of your obscurations. It is impossible. You must first do the purification yoga, then the repentance yoga, and, after you have received responses from these two practices, you may then do the Jambhala practice. This way, you will receive a

response from the Jambhala. Thank you. [audience applause]

[Q]   Grand Master, how does Ch'an Buddhism [Zen] differ from Vajrayana Buddhism?

[A]   **Many people believe that Ch'an is very easy while Vajrayana Buddhism is very difficult. But, in my opinion, it is just the opposite. In Vajrayana Buddhism, one still has aids in the form of rituals and liturgies. Ch'an has dispensed with rituals and requires one to ascend directly to the realization of Emptiness. Through either Ch'an or Vajrayana Buddhism, one may arrive at Buddhahood in the Present Body.**

I consider Ch'an to be a very high form of Buddhism created by the Chinese. But, to practice Ch'an, one must be able to understand the ultimate meaning of the Ch'an dialogues. For example, what if a guru posed the following situation to us: A little bird is kept inside a bottle and, over time, the bird grows bigger. It is now trapped inside the bottle, and pretty soon it will outgrow the bottle. What can one do if one wants to keep the bird alive and the bottle intact? How would you answer? There is only one solution to this riddle: Such a matter fundamentally does not exist! I don't believe in it at all. Where is one going to find a bird kept inside a bottle? Since it does not exist, one may ignore it.

The Ch'an method is very extraordinary and can bring one great benefits. It concerns itself with the direct ascent from ordinary "personhood" into Buddhahood, without climbing any "staircase" in between. Vajrayana Buddhism, on the other hand, provides steps in the form of rituals and practices. However, at the final stage of Vajrayana practice, one is, in effect, practicing Ch'an. In the realm of Great Perfection, when one abides in the state of Emptiness, Vajrayana becomes Ch'an. Thank you.

[Q]   Grand Master, after receiving the internal fire empowerment, I have started to do the practice. Perhaps it is because I am an older student, but my blood pressure has gone up since I started. Lately I have also had the sensation that my whole body is being burnt by fire. Are these symptoms related to the fact that I am older? Should an older person take some precaution or refrain from this practice?

[A]   **It is true that some people find that their blood pressure goes up when they do the Precious Vase Chi Practice, or they feel a fiery chi inside their bodies when they do the Internal Fire Practice. This is because the concentration of mental energy has caused a rise in one's body temperature. But, during these practices, one must be able to control and regulate such phenomena. In other words, when it is too hot, one has to visualize water from a cool lake** dripping down upon one's head, or the refreshing nectar from a Buddha or Bodhisattva coming down to lower the fire. One cannot just have fire; one must be able to coordinate fire with water to transform it into a state of coolness.

Therefore, just doing the Internal Fire Practice without coordinating the descent of the nectar (the merging of fire with water) can be dangerous. If you are unable to tamp down this impetuous fire, you may develop toothache, red and swollen eyes, migraine headache, or even skin diseases. The method used by Vajrayana is to have the internal fire and the nectar from the thousand-petalled-lotus chakra merge together at the heart chakra. Thank you.

[Q]   Grand Master, can you tell us what the future of Texas will be? [audience laughter]

[A]   I want to share with you something that I have experienced on this trip that was a first for me. I have lived half a century and, for the first time while I was having a meal, there were security guards patrolling outside. Because of this necessity, plus the fact that the Chinese translation for "Texas" is "the Virtue State," I feel that the emphasis for everyone here is the word "virtue." With virtue, there will be a great future for Texas. Without virtue, one will live in trembling fear. For the last couple days, I haven't been able to eat peacefully. [audience laughter]

[Q]   Grand Master, please teach us the Sitatapatre [the Great White Parasol Buddha Mother] Practice.

[A]   **Transmitting a practice is no simple matter, and you wait till now to ask this question!** [audience laughter] **On this sheet of paper is the liturgy of the Sitatapatre practice. Generally, the main body of a Tantric liturgy consists of the mudra, mantra, and visualization. This is the mudra for Sitatapatre, and it resembles a parasol. One may visualize a white Empty Space from which the seed syllable "Om" is generated. It rotates to become Sitatapatre. The long mantra is: "Om, Sarwa, Tathagata, Ahnica, Sida, Dataga, Hum pei, Hum mama, Hum ni, Soha." The short mantra is: "Hum mama, Hum ni, Soha."**

Earlier a student asked a question about being weighed down by ghosts during sleep. Doing the Sitatapatre practice can eliminate this problem. At the start, do a complete set of seven Sitatapatre practices, then repeat a single practice twice a month. The Sitatapatre practice can help one avoid various kinds of disasters. Listed here on this paper are the sixteen kinds of benefits associated with this practice.

How long does the effect of performing a sacred boundary last? Initially, a Tantric practitioner should do one practice a day for seven days. A

complete set is comprised of seven practices. After that, repeat the practice twice a month or every fifteen days to maintain the power of protection. The formula for a Tantric ritual consists of the integration of visualization, mudra, and mantra.

The Sitatpatre offers extraordinary merits. Here they are listed as: 1) Like the lion's roar, the outpouring of great compassion from Buddhas can bring auspiciousness, peace, and happiness. 2) Eradication of all obscurations and transgressions of sentient beings. 3) The mantra can magnetize all mantras and has the incomparably ferocious power to strike down all obstructions. 4) the assembly of countless and limitless blessings from Buddhas, as numerous as the Ganges sand. 5) Great joy will arise in the Twenty Eight Constellation Deities. 6) Great joy will arise in the eighty-four thousand beings in the vajra mandala and their protection will be extended. Well, I won't read the rest. There are altogether sixteen merits and benefits in doing the Sitatapatre practice. [see footnote for the rest of the merits] The complete liturgy can be found in my books, and I have also given a detailed teaching of this practice at the Tantric Buddhist Society in Richmond, British Columbia.

Master Samantha: This concludes the question and answer session. We are extremely grateful to and appreciative of Grand Master for compassionately answering all these questions. [applause] The Principal Deity of this Dharma Ceremony is the compassionate Kuan Yin Bodhisattva. When one's heart becomes like Kuan Yin's, one will be moved by great compassion to help and bring benefits to all sentient beings. Mee Yee Tong has prepared a song to sing the praises of the greatly compassionate Kuan Yin. Let us join together to sing praises to the benevolence, compassion, joy, and equanimity of Kuan Yin Bodhisattva. Thank you.

Footnote: The rest of the merits engendered by the Sitatapatre practice are: 7) Reading into one's fate. 8) Rebirth to Sukhavati. 9) Eradication of illness and pain in humans or animals. 10) Attraction of harmony and respect to one, wherever one goes, as all negative forces will be turned away. 11) Elimination of all black magic put upon one. 12) Dispelling of all nightmares and aid in disasters caused by poisoning, weapons, fire, or flood. 13) The impure ones will become pure, and the non-penitent ones will become penitent. 14) If involved in warfare, the mantra can speedily restore the border to a peaceful state. 15) If a woman desires a male child, she will give birth to a male of wisdom. 16) All devas and nagas will bring favorable weather in accordance with the seasons.

Chapter 6

A Word from Master in 1995

The Purple Lotus Temple, a local branch of the True Buddha School, was founded eight years ago in the San Francisco Bay Area. This journey of three thousand days has been one interwoven with blood, sweat, and tears.

On May 2nd 1987, His Holiness Living Buddha Lian-sheng promulgated the establishment of the Purple Lotus Temple. At that moment, I understood that leading other sentient beings aboard the "dharma vessel" was a responsibility I could not decline, even if it meant the giving up of my personal concerns, my family, and my life.

It was a task I felt morally obligated to undertake.

This conviction is just as strong today. The enthusiasm I felt that day eight years ago still pulsates powerfully through my veins. It motivates me to work arduously and whole-heartedly for the development and growth of the organization.

I would like to take this opportunity to thank my husband, Andrew Chou. Eight years ago, he asked me to sign a contract with the statement: "I am willingly assuming these responsibilities and will never regret it." If my husband had not forced me to make that commitment to myself, I may not have persevered as I have done.

Eight years ago, with no leadership experience, I tried to convince Andrew to let me use our small living room as a meeting place for other fellow students to do group mediation. He made only one stipulation, "You are choosing this path yourself, so no matter what happens in the future, you must not complain, make any grievances, feel sad, angry, or resentful. You have to assume this responsibility willingly and never regret it." He said that if I were willing to attest to this by signing my name on a contract, I could have the living room for my use. In a moment of determination, I picked up a pen and signed my name on the agreement. Full of confidence, I boasted, "Everything will be fine!"

Little did I know that the signing of my name on this contract would provide me with the motivation needed to keep me on my spiritual path!

Whenever the stress became oppressive, whenever I felt dejected, the words "I am assuming the responsibility willingly and will never regret it" would rise silently to my consciousness. A renewed motivating force would surge forth. Gritting my jaw, straightening my back, I'd spur myself on to accept another round of learning opportunities and challenges. With this newfound courage, I could earnestly and calmly face the task at hand.

Over these eight years, the Purple Lotus Temple has expanded greatly. It now includes a meditation center, a book store that also sells Buddha statues and ritual implements, a vegetarian restaurant, a publishing branch, a multi-media branch, a school, and dormitory. We are currently in the planning stages of building a True Buddha Purple Lotus Temple!

We have had almost one new enterprise each year! At the time, all I could do was to forge ahead and do what needed to be done. I have given all my endeavors my best and left the rest up to the will of the Cosmos! I often tell myself, "Do all that is humanly possible without holding back. When you reach the point where you are doing everything for others, and have not a shred of self concern, the consequences are up to the will of the Cosmos!"

The best proof of this hard work is in the achievements we have accomplished.

I would like to express my deepest and most sincere gratitude to my Root Guru, Vajra Master Sheng-yen Lu. It is through his brightly illuminated guidance that I have been able to orient myself clearly in the right direction and correctly follow the path.

In addition to His Holiness Living Buddha Lian-sheng, I am also truly grateful to the Buddhas of all spaces, all the Nagas, Devas, Dakinis, and Vajra Dharma Protectors who have rendered great support to the Purple Lotus Temple, enabling it to grow and flourish so smoothly!

Last, I want to say "thank you" from the bottom of my heart to all my fellow Vajra students at the Purple Lotus Temple, and to all those around the world who have lent their support throughout the years. May all merits return to all Dharma supporters, may they have good health, great virtue, supreme wisdom, and auspiciousness in all their endeavors!

Chapter 7

Karma
and
Destiny

*A talk by Master Samantha
at Purple Lotus Temple
on April 8, 1997*

Reverends, fellow cultivators, Om Mani Padme Hum, good evening.

For several days, I have been trying to reply to a letter written to me by someone who came across our True Buddha School and wanted answers to his personal problems. The letter is not easy to reply to because it is a narration of the tragic events that have happened in his life. He comes from a large family of ten children. His father died of cancer, one of his elder brothers died very young, and another died in an automobile accident. Both his first and fourth sisters are divorced, his second sister is always quarrelling with her husband, and the third sister's business is in a slump. Anyway, none of his siblings are happy. His mother is a gambler and does not take care of the family. Through attending some Buddhist ceremonies and engaging in conversation with some reverends, he has been exposed to Buddhism. Since the concept of fate and destiny is ingrained in traditional Chinese culture, he had asked a Buddhist monk, "Am I having this kind of life because of ill fate?" The monk said to him, "There is no such thing as fate!" This is why he decided to write to me to ask, "Does fate exist after all? Is there destiny? Can this predestined fate be changed?"

After reading the account of his family, one indeed sympathizes with him. None of the ten siblings is happy or having a smooth life. He even talks about frequent dreams in which he sees his deceased father and brothers in shabby clothes and in very poor conditions.

119

During the annual Pure Brightness (Memorial) Festival, his family would only allow the tending of his father's grave, while ignoring the grave of the brother who died young. They do this because one feng shui professional had told them, "Those who die before reaching maturity will bring bad luck to the family if they are disturbed. It is sufficient to just bury them. Do not tend to the grave or reclaim their bones, or you will risk bad luck to the family."

On visits to the grave sites, he feels sorry to see his brother's grave covered by wildly grown weeds, but he cannot pull them or make any incense offering. His mother considers such acts unlucky. He wrote, "We have not tended to his grave at all. There are already so many problems in our family, will tending to him or helping him really make our problems worse?" In his letter, he listed all kinds of questions related to his family members: Why the divorces? Why the fatal car accident? Why the quarrelling and fighting within the family? Why…? Just holding the pen in my hand and thinking about these questions gave me a headache. I should emulate our Guru in that, when someone asks many questions, he picks only one to answer. I usually try to answer all ten if ten questions are posed and that takes up too much time.

Why is it that some Buddhist reverends claim that Buddhism does not believe in fate or destiny? This is because Shakyamuni Buddha wants to teach sentient beings that fate can be transcended. If one told the masses that fate exists and that everything is predestined, then people would become very discouraged and pessimistic. Why bother if everything is predestined! People would have a grayish outlook on life and lose the desire to overcome difficult situations or crises.

But, of course, fate exists. Fate is, in fact, karma, so how can there be no fate? Destiny, which is a succession of fates, exists. Take, for example, the turtle that one of you has brought here tonight and was just now making a lot of noise. Fate also exists for it. You should have put it on a tray instead of keeping it inside the paper bag. Although I cannot see it, it was continually making sounds to make itself known to us.

It is also fate that this turtle was born as an animal. Why is this so? Just now, when I entered into samadhi during the Bardo Deliverance, I decided to investigate why the turtle was born into the animal realm. In its previous human life, he and his father's family were in the business of making and selling cakes. They were hard workers. But on one occasion, when they found out that another baker had made a large purchase of flour, he and his father decided to steal it. With minimal effort, they stole all the flour and moved it to their own bakery. The other baker had spent almost all he owned in acquiring the flour and had to declare bankruptcy because of the theft. In those times, there was no such thing as insurance reimbursement for stolen property, so he lost everything and, as a result, he lived very unhappily. After running into many stone walls, he ultimately committed suicide by hanging. On the other hand, the family that had stolen the flour acquired the raw material without spending any money, and by knocking out a competitor, they were able to expand their business and become very rich.

Due to this past theft, the baker's son had to be born this life in the form of an animal with truncated limbs. He retracts and hides his head, hands, and feet, unable to extend them. These are the reasons for this. After committing the theft, the baker's son knew in his heart that he had caused a great deal of suffering for the other baker and his family. But what was done was done, so what could he do? How could he admit his crime, confessing to the other man, "I have stolen all your flour!" It was not possible! So, because of that mistake, by creating that karmic cause, the man will be born as an animal several dozen times and, even when born again as a human, will live very short lives.

While the turtle was there making all these noises, I asked the Bodhisattva, "Since it has created such a karmic cause in its past life to be born as a turtle, what is the cause then for it to come to a Buddhist temple in this life and to participate in a group cultivation, receiving blessings from a Bardo Deliverance Ceremony? Was he a spiritual cultivator before?" The Bodhisattva said, "No, he has not done any spiritual practice. But, in that lifetime, he once visited a temple and someone handed him a candle, he took it in his hands and gave the other person some money. Since he had purchased the candle, he lit it and placed it in front of the Buddhas and Bodhisattvas. Because of that one gesture, he has arrived here now.

We may not realize that the lighting of candles is a very great, meritorious act. The offering of a lamp in front of the Buddhas signifies that one has requested the Light, the Buddha Light, to shine on one, to purify the ignorance and darkness within one. When one generates this kind of message in the heart and lights a candle or lamp in front of the Buddhas, the Buddhas and Bodhisattvas shine their light on one in aid. But, in this life, the turtle had to be born into the animal realm to pay back for the wrong he had done. Such is fate. What is created in a past life will result in consequences in a later life.

Shakyamuni Buddha teaches us to transcend karma. Karma exists, but it does not mean there is no way out, for there are ways to rise above it. Practice spiritual cultivation, and practice continually. When you cultivate to reach and realize Emptiness, you will be free from the bondage of karma, the forces of yin and yang and the five elements, and you will no longer be subjected to the laws of heaven and earth and of gods and ghosts. When you have risen above those laws, you will no longer be subjected to the laws of karma and destiny. That is why some Buddhists deny the existence of fate and destiny. It is also the major reason why some Buddhist monks flatly deny it. They want to encourage us to stay focused on the goal of cultivation. Otherwise, if we encounter a little difficulty or slandering, we immediately lose our equilibrium; if we suffer a little injustice, we are immediately thrown into a state of disorder and want to file grievances. It is very difficult for a person reacting in such ways to attain Emptiness.

What Shakyamuni Buddha has taught us is that the Buddhadharma we have today may indeed help us to cultivate to transcend all kinds of bondage and rise above karma.

Hui-ke, the second patriarch of Zen after Bodhidharma, is an example of someone who rose above karma. He cultivated to a very high fruition level, but do you know how his life ended? He was decapitated! He died of capital punishment. What a terrible ending for a lineage master! Could he have failed in his cultivation? Did he lack the ability to divert such a retribution? Did he not have any transcendental power? Of course he had the power. Take a look again at Mahamaudgalyayana, one of the ten chief disciples of Shakyamuni Buddha. As Mahamaudgalyayana was known for his supreme transcendental power, his power was limitless. He could travel to the Buddhas' Purelands to hear discourses, and to the realm of hell to save his mother. He could travel freely within the Ten Dharma Realms. But how did he die? He was crushed to the ground by falling boulders. What a horrible death! Shariputra was known for his supreme wisdom, but how did he die? He died of displacement of his intestines. All these individuals attained realization through cultivation, yet their deaths were tragic. We might say, "Their cultivation did not seem to have helped them as they were unable to escape their fates. I don't want to be like them. I want to be able to die in a serene sitting posture with plenty of sariras found in my cremated remains..."

In the past, I have explained that although they had the power to escape their fates, they chose, however, to demonstrate to us that when the karmic cause was one of a severe transgression, such as killing, they eventually had to face the consequences. Mahamaudgalyayana has shown us that he was able to foil several attempts on his life when he detoured from paths when enemies with rocks had been waiting in ambush. But why did he not escape that last time? Because he had attained self-mastery and freedom. During the time of experiencing the punishment, he was abiding in a heart of great bliss when receiving the retribution, without any hatred or blame.

When I was delivering my son Engih, I developed severe hemorrhaging. The doctors were not immediately able to locate the source of bleeding. They repeatedly gave me transfusions, but I continued losing blood. It was a kind of retribution that I had to lose all the blood in my body. I had to have my abdomen cut open, and many organs taken out. I have been born as the incarnation [of the Purple Lotus] and have engaged in my practice, so why did I have to experience retribution? It was fate, and I had to take responsibility for my own karma.

Therefore, there are situations wherein a person who has attained the state of Emptiness, upon facing a karmic consequence, willingly accepts it. He uses the situation to teach us to face up to our own karma instead of running away from it, and also to show us that, after acquiring mastery over birth and death, he can depart from this human world in whatever way he chooses. He is free to experience or not experience the retribution. Such a person must, however, have already attained the wisdom of Emptiness.

When one is in possession of the wisdom of Emptiness, one abides in a state of supreme bliss. No matter how perilous the situation, such a person accepts it happily. I would like to tell everyone today that a truly accomplished adept is able to rise above any circumstance and is not bound by the laws of heaven and earth, gods and ghosts, yin and yang, the five elements, or karma. Such an adept is able to completely release all of these laws into Emptiness and, at the same time, abide in a very happy state. Therefore, fate and destiny exist, but by following Shakyamuni Buddha's teachings, we can transcend them. There is a way to transcend them and it has to do with the opening of your heart and mind: whatever you are facing, be completely aware of the situation and happily accept it.

During my surgery, when the doctor was removing many organs from my body, my bladder became filled with blood and my intestines swollen. Since I was not able to urinate on my own, the doctor had catheterized me. I was not aware of this procedure because the catheter was inserted during surgery. In any case, all I knew after the surgery was that I woke up and was able to live again. Eight weeks later, the doctor told me that he had to take out the tubing. I thought to myself, "Another surgery!" My body was still weak and in much pain from the last surgery. I asked the doctor, "What kind of tubing are you talking about?" He said, "It is a plastic tubing." "How long?" I asked. "This long," he said and lifted up a plastic tubing to show me. How big? It was almost the same size as a human finger. Such a long and thick tubing inside my body! I asked the doctor, "Another surgery, does this mean another incision? How long will this take?" There was already a long incision going from my upper to the lower abdomen. He said, "There is no need for surgery." I said, "No surgery? Then how are you going to take it out?" He said, "We will take it out from the opening of the urethra." As soon as I heard that, I almost fainted. I thought, "Wouldn't that be very painful? This is a body made of flesh! Such a long and thick plastic tubing inside the body and it has to be pulled out from where you pee?"

The doctor went on, "It will be done without any anesthesia while you are awake. It won't require any incision." Just the thought of it drained the strength from my limbs. Fear of pain! It was a very natural reaction because I had been in pain every day and knew what it was like to be in pain. Then he asked me to get up on the operating table, and started to get himself ready for the procedure. First he took out a small alcohol pad to disinfect the area, and next he took out a stainless steel vajra scepter-like instrument to keep the urethra dilated so the tubing could be pulled out. All this was to be done without anesthesia.

I was lying there on the table and, before the procedure could begin, tears gushed from my eyes and I sobbed miserably. The nurse said, "It will be over very quickly. You will be all right; the pain only lasts for a brief moment. Don't be afraid. The doctor does this all the time; it will be very quick. It won't hurt for long." I asked, "How long will it hurt?" She said, "A few minutes." When one is in pain, several seconds, or even one second, can be an intolerable duration, let alone several minutes. I started crying out loud.

Dharma brother Chou [Andrew, Master's husband] was by my side and tried to console me, "She said it won't take more than a moment. It won't hurt too long! It is still better than having another surgery." I said, "Take a look at that dilator and the way it rotates. It is as big as an egg beater!" I wasn't crying from fear, but they kept on telling me, "Do not be afraid!" I said, "I am not crying because I am afraid, I am crying because I am penitent." All of a sudden, I was so repentant that I started wailing. I thought to myself, "What wrongs had I committed? What kinds of transgressions had I done that I now was to receive this kind of retribution? What crimes had I done in previous lives that I had to receive this kind of physical torture and suffering?" I cried out to

Kuan Yin Bodhisattva, "Whatever I did in past lives, I won't dare to commit them anymore. Please help me so I will be able to live this life in full awareness of my actions. Help me so I won't be so ignorant as to continue creating negative karma. I won't and I don't dare create any more negative karma for my body to suffer such retribution again. When this is over, I am going to live righteously and purely."

At that moment, I broke down and wept in grief. The others in the room were at a loss to why I would cry like that. But, in that one moment, I was overwhelmed by the realization that the suffering created by one's own karma could be so intense that nothing could take its place and that no one other than oneself could feel it. When this was on my mind, I spoke to the Bodhisattva, "I will willingly accept whatever retribution I deserve. I will undergo it to neutralize the karma."

Then, in that moment, after willingly facing and accepting the karmic retribution, my heart opened up. With my heart open, I chanted the Buddha's name and visualized the Buddhas and Bodhisattvas empowering me. In a flash, I forgot about the pain. I watched the instrument going in to dilate the urethra, and I watched the tubing being located and pulled out. It was this long, almost the length this desk! I still have it as a memento. It is hard to imagine how it could have been squeezed in, but it was flexible and had been there all that time to help drain the urine.

It really didn't hurt. I had completely released myself in that one moment and was happy to face the retribution and to have it neutralized. If I had not had to undergo the crisis, how would I ever have been able to neutralize the wrongs I had committed in the past? In that moment I rose above the psychological roadblock and felt happy. It was a kind of training experience. And ever since, during the following eight years, whenever I have come across any negative or perilous situation, I have looked upon it as a chance for me to neutralize my negative karma. How else can one ever pay back one's debt? One may not know specifically what kinds of debts one has created, but one may look upon one's suffering as a means to pay back and neutralize the debts. When one thinks this way, one's perspective is changed and any crisis can be transcended.

Therefore, Shakyamuni Buddha teaches that only by opening up the knots in one's heart and by releasing one's mind into Emptiness may one transcend the suffering of one's destiny. When the laws of yin and yang and the five elements no longer bind one, one may go freely east, west, north, south, up or down. The words of feng shui professionals can no longer bind one, neither can anyone's intimidating words. Certain elements considered inauspicious in a household, such as the placement of a stove across from the sink, the presence of too many sharp angles, absence of a "wealth spot," or the bed facing the doorway, can no longer exert any adverse effects on one. Before, one was bound by such laws and their influences. Now one has transcended these obstacles and is completely free of them. The incompatible elements of fire and water in a house have nothing to do with one; the presence of an edge of a wall facing the front door has nothing to do with one; a gaping hole at the wealth spot has nothing to do with one; and the positioning of the bed right across the doorway has nothing to do with one. This happens because one has risen above the laws of destiny and karma and is completely free.

All these are the things I would very much like to tell this friend who has written to me. But how? Time and space is limited, so I can only dedicate merits to him in my meditations and assign him homework to do. Through this kind of homework [chanting of mantras and sutras, charitable work, etc.] and through self reflection and contemplation, one may gain a new perspective and new understanding to rise above one's difficulties. When one is no longer controlled by the various kinds of fates, one is a person who has realized the nature of Emptiness. May you all succeed in that realization.

Om Mani Padme Hum.

Chapter 8

Key to
Enlightenment

*An excerpt of a Dharma talk
given by Master Samantha
at Purple Lotus Temple
on September 13, 1997*

Reverends, fellow cultivators, Om Mani Padme Hum, good evening.

Earlier, Rev. Lian-kai reported that, among the many sutras printed by the Purple Lotus Temple for free distribution, there is one entitled "The Buddha Speaks the Dharani Sutra of Long Life." In my consultations, I have come across many cases, with both students and non-students, of those who have had abortions, miscarriages, or lost a child and subsequently experienced interference and distress in their lives. In the past I always advised them to do practices and to register the baby or child for Bardo services. I have even asked them to consult the divination blocks to determine if they should install a plaque in the name of the deceased in the Ksitigarbha Room [a room at PLS dedicated for such purposes]. This is one way to provide psychological relief to someone who suffers from guilt or is still haunted by the experience.

For some time I have urged people to print this sutra because of the great benefits generated from doing so. One time, a lady came with her husband for a consultation. She was educated and had a well paying job. Both she and her husband were engineers working in the San Francisco Bay Area. Her problem was that they did not have any children, so she came to ask me if anything could be done.

I closed my eyes to pray to Kuan Yin Bodhisattva for guidance. As soon as I closed my eyes, I saw a little boy, about ten years old, standing by her side, tugging at her dress, and calling her "mama." I was surprised, as she was childless and had come to ask for help in getting pregnant.

I asked her, "Have you ever given birth before?" She replied, "No, I have never had any children." I responded, "Then why am I seeing a little boy, around the age of ten, standing next to you and holding onto your hand and calling you mama?"

As soon as I finished speaking, the couple looked at each other, and the wife broke down, sobbing loudly. She told me, "When I was younger and studying as a foreign student, I got pregnant. Because of finances and circumstances at that time, we felt we could not have raised the child so I had an abortion. This was ten years ago, and I have not been able to get pregnant since then." It was indeed ten years ago when she had had the abortion. Surprisingly and unbeknownst to her, this invisible child has been following her around for ten years.

There are many cases like hers. We could only ask her to do practices to help herself, or perform Bardo Deliverance services to provide help and guidance for the spirit to be reborn. Now, this sutra spoken by Shakyamuni Buddha twenty-five hundred years ago informs us that, when in such a predicament, one can print this sutra and enough merits will be generated to lead the deceased to rebirth.

Sometimes, the problem is caused by a family member who has had miscarriages or abortions. I came across the case of a young girl in my counseling who had never been married or dated and had not had any abortions or miscarriages herself, but whose mother had had a previous miscarriage. The aborted fetus would have been her older brother, and its spirit was running around amongst the siblings, causing disharmony and disrupting their normal growth and development. From the spirit's point of view, he was thinking, "Why couldn't I have come into this world like the rest of you?" Not so long ago, families with too many children sometimes had an unwanted pregnancy terminated as a means of family planning. The spirit of the aborted fetus would sometimes stay around to cause trouble. This is what was happening in her case.

In such cases, we can help by printing this sutra. It may be one's mother, one's sisters or sisters-in-law who have had abortions or miscarriages. We may still help them this way. Otherwise, spirits may cause disruptions within the family. This happens because the child to be born may retain a karmic tie with oneself for decades. One can prevent the child from being born into the physical realm, but karmic affinity still exists in the invisible realm. The being will hang around next to one or run around inside one's body. If one owes the child a karmic debt, then the child may try to collect in an invisible way, because a physical means was denied.

It is, therefore, an excellent idea to print this sutra, which is only a very slim book. A long time ago, I urged people to print it, but this had not been carried out until now. There is a need for its printing because modern medical procedures and easy accessibility have made abortions more available.

There was even one case which involved a man who came to ask for consultation. He was afflicted with a strange illness which doctors could not cure. Around a certain time each year, he would be stricken by an abdominal pain so severe that he felt as if he were being stabbed. He would then start bleeding. It was a frightening experience, but medical examinations turned up nothing. After looking into the matter, it turned out that he had had many girl friends and had been sleeping around a lot. Unbeknownst to him, one of the women had become pregnant. The woman knew that the man was not going to take any responsibility, as he had clearly indicated that he was not going to marry her. She subsequently had an abortion and felt a lot of anger towards him.

The woman had originally wanted to keep the child but, after deeply considering the matter, had concluded that she could not afford the child on her own. She finally went for an illegal abortion in her fifth month of pregnancy. At that stage, the baby was well formed. When there is great grievance in an aborted fetus, it looks for the source of its own demise.

Many of these workings are not apparent to us, and this is why we have to print this sutra. Printing this sutra and repenting for the mistakes we have made, can help bring closure to the matter. It is most effective when one prints, distributes, and chants the sutra. If one just distributes it, without any helping with the printing or without chanting, one only receives one third of the merits. When one carries out all three aspects as stated in the True Buddha Sutra, blessed are the ones who chant, print, and distribute the sutra.

****

The Purple Lotus Temple shall help print books, such as repentance liturgies, that benefit modern men. Having a copy of a repentance liturgy in one's home, is like having an heirloom. Sincerely reading the repentance liturgy, which lists all kinds of transgressions, is tantamount to confessing and repenting for all of the transgressions one has committed from time immemorial. It will lead to the diminishing and eradication of karmic hindrances.

The first time I participated in this particular repentance ceremony was in August of 1997 [the Emperor Liang Repentacne held in Ling Shen Ching Tze Temple in Redmond, August 25-29, 1997, prior to the annual Bardo Ceremony]. Although some fellow cultivators have suggested that we practice this repentance, we have never given it a try at the Purple Louts Temple since it is so long. To be honest, practicing the Emperor Liang Repentance requires not just mental, but also physical stamina. The Great Compassion Repentance and Water Repentance are, in comparison, much shorter. Among all repentance ceremonies, the Emperor Liang Repentance is the longest and most physically demanding, taking three to seven days to complete.

I brought Megia with me on this trip to practice the repentance ceremony. The first morning session was begun by Grand Master, and many masters were present. There were two sessions each day with a break in between. Since Grand Master had to take care of business in the True Buddha Tantric Quarter, he left after the first session and told all the masters, "These sessions are not obligatory. Anyone who has time and wants to stay may stay. If you find it too demanding, you may skip it." Grand Master made it clear that the decision was completely up to us.

After lunch, I went to the motel to pick up a few things, then hurried back to the temple. When I arrived, I took a look and saw that, of the several dozen masters present in the morning, only Master Li, Master Lai, and I had returned. Master Lai was asked to join the men at one side, and Master Li and I stayed with the other women at the other side. This was what happened during the second session. At the third session, Master Lai was nowhere to be seen, only Master Li and I remained. I told Master Li, "You have to be brave and stick it out. Don't let me be the only one left. I have come especially for this ceremony, why has everyone disappeared?" She said, "No, no. I will stay till the end." However, on the third day she was not able to kneel anymore and could only remain seated. While others were kneeling, she had to sit. Her chronic back pain had struck and she had to sit on three cushions to ease the pain.

I tried to encourage her, "You must persist!" She said, "Don't worry, I will keep you company." I stayed through all the sessions. Starting with the first session, by entering into a true mode of confession, I was able to see the workings of karma and reincarnations and how obscurations and hindrances arise. Shakyamuni Buddha has told us that karmic hindrances have prevented us from seeing clearly. Our present conditions are results of previous actions. There are karmic causes behind one's wealth or poverty, functional or dysfunctional family, high or low intelligence, and luck or misfortune. All these are listed in great detail in the repentance liturgy. Every transgression in words, thoughts, or deeds may result in karmic retribution.

For example, we have many offerings here at the shrine. After a while, these offerings must be brought downstairs to the dining room. Perhaps a student or reverend, seeing some food item he or she likes, decides to hide the item for his or her personal use. Even such an act is listed in the repentance liturgy as a transgression which one needs to confess and repent. Isn't it terrifying!

Some of the things listed would not have occurred to you to be transgressions, until you read about them. For example, say we are sitting here now and thirsty, and we ask Rev. Lian-kai to go downstairs to bring us some bottled water. Or, in the olden days, we would have asked him to draw some water for us. He would say, "Fine, I will be responsible for drawing the water." After drawing the water and, as he was bringing the bucket up for us, it might occur to him to have some. "My mouth is so dry, let me first take a sip." It is quite terrifying that such a simple action constitutes a transgression! You have been delegated to go and draw the water for everyone. Therefore, the water belongs to everyone and you owe it to everyone to notify them first before drinking the water.

How can one exist without making any errors? You may say to yourself, "I have not beaten, cursed, or killed anyone, and I have a good heart." But, when taking a sip of water this way creates a karmic transgression, how can one be immune from making any errors at all? Reading this in the repentance liturgy struck terror in me. The accidental errors one commits are just too numerous. How can one ever wash them away! It is impossible!

Contained in this thick volume of Emperor Liang Repentance are all kinds of karmic transgressions. An error may take only a few seconds to commit, yet its consequence can impact one's life in one, several, or even numerous lives to come.

Last week I told you a story of Shakyamuni Buddha which happened during one of his reincarnations. Although Shakyamuni became the Buddha in one life, it does not mean he was extraordinary in all his lives. Last time, during the Red

Jambhala fire puja, the Red Jambhala revealed to me that there were karmic ties between him and me. I had been his teacher in one of my previous lives. While it may sound extraordinary, it is in fact a very simple matter. If anything, it shows how great Red Jambhala is. He is not bound by transmigrations while I have to go through transmigrations. Therefore, I am in a more sorrowful state than he is. He was reveling in joy while we were doing the fire puja.

Before becoming the Buddha, Shakyamuni Buddha led lives of wickedness, destructiveness, as animals and hell beings. One time, he was in the realm of hells and had to wear around his head a very hot and burning ring. The burning made him cry out in pain. He asked the official administering punishment, "Why is this happening to me?" The official said, "Quiet down and look back to your previous lives to see what you have done." Since he had a deep root of wisdom, he was able to quiet down to look for the cause.

In another life, he was someone who had relished killing and was easily provoked into doing so. His mother abhorred such behavior and tried to dissuade him. One day, his mother decided to hide his slaughter knife. When he noticed his knife missing, he became angry. After a long search, he finally found it behind his mother, who was taking a nap. He was so upset that he decided to step over her to retrieve the knife. Just as he was picking up the knife, he accidentally stepped on her head. The pain woke her up, as the weight of a grown man could be tremendous. He did not feel he had done anything wrong and chided her, "Why have you hidden my knife?" Without waiting for an answer, he ran off.

Just this one act caused him, after finally exhausting his blessings, to descend to the realm of hells and suffer the retribution of having a burning ring around his head. Isn't it horrifying?

Shakyamuni Buddha has lived many other lives apart from the one in which he attained Buddhahood, and he definitely has had many teachers and formed many karmic ties in those other lives. So it is not so strange when the Red Jambhala said that I once had been his teacher.

Red Jambhala has a great affinity with us and, one of these days, I must tell him, "You are so joyful, please help us to become just as joyful. Do not dance and revel in joy by yourself! We would like to attain the same level as you and be a Joyful Deva." If one does not yet have the ability to be a Buddha, then one should be a Joyful Deva. Wouldn't it be wonderful if everyone were happy and joyful?

The force of karmic retribution is tremendous. This is why it is necessary to participate at repentance liturgies. By gaining the understanding and learning what kind of retribution follows certain actions, one may avoid indulging in unwholesome speech, thoughts, and actions. This is of utmost importance. Otherwise, one will declare, "I don't care." I often hear people say they don't care. People may think they do not care, but retribution can change people's minds.

****

During my near death experience eight years ago in 1990, when I almost hemorrhaged to death, my spirit traveled to an upper spiritual realm. Grand Master stopped me and asked me to return to the human realm because my mission in the world was not finished. I refused, "It is so liberating to be able to leave, please do not make me go back to all that suffering." I had not committed suicide, and I was just having my karmic retributions neutralized. Although it was an ugly death to lose all of one's blood, it was a result of my own actions. In previous lives, I had committed too many killings. Having been a general, a king, and a leader, how many lives had been terminated as a result of my command? Of course I had to pay the debt and balance the karma; therefore, I accepted my death with great willingness.

But Grand Master insisted that I come back. I tried to defy him. After all, being in the spiritual realm endows one with a power greater than one has on earth. I tried my best to resist returning.

He said, "Come back, there are all these tasks that need to be done." I decided to have a preview of what I would encounter when I returned. After spreading open the clouds, I took a look and was petrified by the pervasive darkness below. While it was bright in the upper worlds, the realms below were completely shrouded in blackness. What a challenge it would be to try to push the blackness to one side and find a path for oneself and others to follow! Everything was darkness, like ink spilled from a bottle staining everything it touched. My job was to pave the way for sentient beings to find the path to the Light. What an arduous task! How could one go about such a task?

Of course, after seeing such a scene, I ran away. I made up my mind that I would not come back. However, as I have said many times before, I had no choice but to come back. Why? Because my power was not as great as Grand Master's. He has cultivated to a level higher than I. He is a Buddha and has attained full realization. I had nothing. It took him no time at all to toss me into the world again. It was that simple. He just picked me up and dropped me back.

That was why, after I was rescued, I went to say thank you and prostrate to him. I told him that I would work very hard, so that next time, when I needed to make my escape, he would not be able to stop me. I also acknowledged to him that he knew that I was really not qualified to ascend yet. I would only be fit for a door-keeper there. After all, there are many rungs on the ladders in the spiritual realm. One goes to the level appropriate for one based on one's merits, level of realization, and spiritual power. Not everyone who returns becomes a Buddha or Bodhisattva. At that time I had only taken refuge a few years earlier, I had not done much and my understanding was not profound. Of course I would be assigned to the level that befitted me. I would have to climb the ladder step by step. Grand Master was actually very compassionate in bringing me back, allowing me another chance to work harder, so that the next time around I could run faster and would not be a door-keeper.

After returning, I have realized that I am in a war zone full of land mines. It is so treacherous that any misstep can blow me into smithereens. All kinds of situations, if not handled correctly, are potential explosive land mines. That is why I must be very careful and alert. Before any mission here is accomplished, I absolutely must take my task seriously and not step on those land mines.

****

Earlier, Rev. Lian-yang talked about not making any mental discrimination between one's job and other people's jobs. If one understands the true meaning of human existence, one will very naturally do whatever business needs to be done. One will not think, "No one has asked me to do this," or "it is below me to do it." Very naturally, one regards every task that needs to be done as one's own task. It is the recoiling of self and the comparison of self to others that gives rise to disputes and emotional distress. When one regards every job as one's job, then the problem is solved. Things are much simpler when disparate thoughts are focused into one single thought.

A while ago a fellow student told me her grievances. She felt that she cared a lot for others and often times reached out her hand first, but others did not reciprocate. This saddened her. What were the causes of the problem? Were those fellow students who rejected her to blame? I told her, "The problem lies in being suspicious." She said, "Right, right, they are too suspicious of me." I said, "No, it is you who are suspicious of them. It is mutual suspicion." A person's suspicion can create many unfortunate and regrettable situations.

Basically, when you do not engender any thoughts of suspicion, your life will be much simpler. Even if it is clear that another person dislikes you, do not dwell on it. Instead, receive and embrace him with smiles and extended arms. He may be very mean and try to hurt you, but there will come a day when he feels that you are the loveliest and friendliest among this whole group of people. At the end, he will even become your best friend.

I have a very good Dharma Protector helping me. Over these last several years of cultivation and propagating the Buddhadharma, there have been many negative rumors circulating about me. My best Dharma Protector has completely shielded my hearing and seeing faculties from all these rumors while they took place. I was not affected and was able to remain focused on my goal. It was when the task was almost complete that I started to hear about rumors which had circulated two to three years before. By then they had become things of the past and could no longer cause me any pain.

For example, say I was to pour a cup of water for you to drink and someone started a rumor that I had poisoned the water to kill you or inflict you with diarrhea. If I had learned of such an accusation before pouring the water into your cup, I would be wounded. Before offering you this water to relieve your thirst, I would have been discouraged and discarded the water.

It was with a heart of joy I offered to relieve everyone's thirst. If I had learned that my intention was misunderstood, I would have stopped pouring the water to put down the rumors. The Dharma Protectors were wonderful in turning off my hearing faculty. I was completely unaware of all those rumors and happily continued urging others to drink, "Have a cup!" Everyone's thirst was relieved. Then, a couple of years later, when I heard talk of "poison in the water," it no longer meant anything.

Therefore, being unaware of current rumors has its advantage. It allows me to be more focused on the task of teaching the Buddhadharma. I am very grateful to the Buddhas, Bodhisattvas, and Dharma Protectors for keeping me from being disturbed, so I may remain positive and energetic in reaching our goal.

I always pray to them to give me such opportunities so I may carry out my task fearlessly, without regret, until I attain Buddhahood. You should pray for such opportunities, otherwise, it is useless to say, "I vow to deliver sentient beings, three of them or thirty of them, each year." If you make such vows, you must act upon them. Pick something up for someone you meet at dinner or for someone at the shopping mall who has dropped something and give a helping hand to someone not feeling well—all these are opportunities for you to carry out your vow. A power will be generated when a vow is carried out. Vows not acted upon bear a heavy interest penalty.

Earlier, in meditation, the Buddhas and Bodhisattvas told me, "Tell everyone the key to Enlightenment." Do you know what the key to Enlightenment is? The goal of the True Buddha School practices is to attain "Enlightenment and Liberation." How does one attain Enlightenment, the innate Heart and Buddha Nature? Understand that every practice has its own key.

The Buddhas and Bodhisattvas asked me to tell you the key to Enlightenment without providing me with the answer. This indicates that they think I know the answer. The answer is quite simple. Just these eight words: "I am the Buddha, the Buddha is I."

It is just this simple. Experience the truth in these words: I am the Buddha. Do not think the Buddha is so high up there that you are being arrogant in making such a consideration. There is no difference between oneself and the Buddha—this is the key to Enlightenment. Contemplate it, then go and practice it. If you just think about it and do not act upon it, it is useless.

I have given you this example before. One time, I was waiting outside a public restroom which had only one toilet. More than a dozen people were in line. It was so stinky in there that everyone was holding her nose when she came out.

When it was my turn, I went in and saw that the toilet bowl had been stopped up, and water mixed with urine and feces overflowed onto the floor. What should one do? There were still a dozen more people waiting outside. The solution is very simple! Take a look at what the problem is. If the toilet is not flushing, something must be blocking the drain hole. Just pull out whatever is stuffed down there. I put my hand into the toilet bowl and scooped out those thick pieces of paper, then I pulled out whatever was blocking the drain hole and threw it into the garbage can. I pressed the lever, and the toilet started flushing. There were paper towels in the restroom, and after using them to do a little clean up, I went to wash my hands. One washing was not enough, and so I washed them two and three times. Well, with that taken care of, I was able to use the restroom myself, and everyone after me could also use it. How simple! This is spiritual cultivation. It is just this simple.

A non-practitioner would not even consider such an unsavory task. But today you are a spiritual cultivator; matters that benefit everyone become your concern. You do not make a distinction between you and others. You ascend the path to seek the Buddha and the Tao, and you descend along the path to help all sentient beings. Only when above, below, and you are aligned in one continuum, are you truly walking on the path. This is something we need to learn, as it is not an understanding with which we are born. You just need to constantly remind yourself and be alert. If you cannot even bring yourself to perform such a service, what else can you do? If you are unable to bring yourself to do a small task such as this, how can you hope to attain Buddhahood which is a billion times more challenging? When urging yourself on, your determination will be firmer. Spiritual cultivation is only possible when your will and determination become progressively stronger.

The path is long with many lessons and tests ahead for your training. You want to pass these tests for your own sake, not because you want to show off your report card to others. When you are truly walking on the path, you will be able to perceive things on a deeper level. Others see only the exterior, but you see beyond the façade. With a wider and deeper perception and a more expansive heart, you will enjoy a great degree of freedom in your life.

Chapter 9

Present Life Karma

A talk by Master Samantha
at the Purple Lotus Temple
on September 29th, 1998.

Several days ago, on Saturday, a couple came to see me for spiritual consultation. It was very late, around midnight, and everyone else had left. They showed up suddenly without any appointment and insisted that they talk to me. Ordinarily we try not to have any consultations after group cultivation, but sometimes there are afternoon appointments that I cannot get to, or we have out of town visitors who come specifically for consultation, and it is quite late by the time I finish.

Intervention Does Not Last Forever

Now when someone facing a severe karmic retribution comes to seek consultation, I no longer immediately pray to the Buddhas and Bodhisattvas for a drastic intervention. Based on personal experience from the last ten years or more, I have learned that karmic hindrances are not neutralized just by using my own spiritual power, or by prayers, the power of the Buddhas, or the blessing or power of the Guru alone.

It is true that the above interventions may work temporarily to stop retribution in its tracks but, if the person in need of help does not have the same kind of understanding, then this kind of help is not appropriate, optimal, or long lasting. To attain long lasting relief, we have to help the person to gain a new understanding, so that from his own heart he will engender a desire to work with the Power of the Spirit.

Otherwise, even if we are able to evict or persuade the attached spirit to leave, it might still return later. Even if the attached spirit in question is delivered to a higher realm through the bardo services we offer, we cannot guarantee that other karmic enemies of the person will stay away from him.

The fact that someone is encountering problems caused by an attached spirit indicates either that he has reached a time in his life when his merits are being exhausted, or that the time for the reckoning of negative karma has come. In such cases, it is very possible that more than one karmic enemy will be waiting at the door. If this person has not developed any power or light in him through meritorious deeds and spiritual cultivation, then, even if the current attached spirit goes away, a different karmic enemy will attach to him tomorrow! Therefore, we have to teach people this kind of knowledge, as it is impossible for us to cradle them or carry them on our backs, protecting them forever.

So now, when I come across such a person, I tell him, "Consult with the divination blocks and see what the Bodhisattvas say." In a way, this is a bargaining process between him and his karmic enemy. First he has to tell the Bodhisattvas what kinds of meritorious deeds he is willing to dedicate himself to doing. If the karmic enemy accepts his offer and is willing to let go of the grudges, then the divination blocks will give a positive reading, and the Bodhisattvas will help him. If the reading is negative, then he needs to increase the amount of meritorious deeds and try the divination blocks again. Lately in my consultations, I tend to use more of this method rather than telling people right away what kinds of homework they should do.

Upper Body Missing

The couple who came that night told me their story, and it was truly a case of present-life karmic retribution. Usually, when people encounter interference from spirits, the spirits are often their ancestors, karmic enemies, or creditors from previous lives. Oftentimes, when people learn that their karma has originated from previous lives, they cannot relate to it emotionally or put much weight into the matter.

The karmic enemies of that couple, however, originated in this present life.

It brings to mind that there are, indeed, great differences between people who do actual spiritual practice and those who don't. You all engage in daily practice and participate in group cultivation and ceremonies, and you read books offering you this kind of knowledge. These activities may not seem that special, but once something out of the ordinary happens, you have more knowledge and resources to help you, and you are able to immediately employ this spiritual knowledge to protect yourself and your family.

Back to the couple who came that night. The husband told me that one day two years ago, while driving across a railway track on his way home, he suddenly felt that two people had got into his car. Each of those two people only had half a body --- their upper bodies were missing. Though he could not see anything when he turned his head to look behind him, he sensed clearly that two people had gotten into his car.

When he got home, he said to his wife, "I feel that two people have been following me home, can you see them?" His wife replied, "No, what two people? There is just you yourself!"

Since it was just a feeling and he could not see them either, it was hard for him to explain to his wife. Soon after that, he suffered a stroke with brain hemorrhage and had to be rushed to the hospital. The doctors performed emergency brain surgery on him. After the surgery, he seemed to have become a different person. He started seeing strange things in the world of the deceased, and slowly he began to lose focus in the living world. His wife attributed these changes to the brain surgery.

Then, he started having aches and pains all over his body. He went through many diagnostic tests including X-rays, blood and urine tests. The results were negative and could not explain why he was feeling ill all over. Daily existence became a torture and at night he could not sleep well at all.

Children in the Nether World

The strangest thing was that, from the underworld, he saw three children calling him "Dad." He did not recognize them, but when they called him "Dad," he felt intuitively that these were his own kids. The oldest child was in his early teens.

Why were there three kids in the underworld calling him Dad? It turned out that in his younger years, due to financial circumstances, his wife had terminated three pregnancies in abortions.

So, you see, the spirits of the aborted fetuses had grown up in the underworld. Since they did not have anyone to look after them, and as soon as they saw this father from the living world, they went to him, crying and running after him for help.

This was why, during this last Bardo Ceremony in Redmond, Grand Master announced that he would like to establish a shrine at the Rainbow Villa specifically dedicated to the spirits of aborted fetuses.

In the underworld, there are many orphans. Since people in the living world do not have this kind of knowledge, they have abortions when they do not want to or cannot afford to raise the child. But the soul of the baby has already descended, and there is nowhere else for him to go. When he has no one to guide him, look after him, or perform Bardo services for him, and when the parents fail to give him a name or recognize him as a member of their genealogy, he becomes an aimless ghost and will often be hanging around the family. Although people in the living world do not know of his existence, when he throws tantrums, he can toss the family into turmoil. This is one of the factors behind family disharmony.

Two Lives Lost

One night, while asleep, the husband's body suddenly started twisting into all kinds of contortions. His wife had been sleeping next to him and asked him, "What are you doing? Why are you moving so violently?" He ignored her. Then, suddenly, he cried out aloud, "All right, I will give you my life! I will give you my life!"

His wife implored him, "What life are you talking about? What is happening?" He still did not wake up and his body continued to move violently.

Suddenly, his wife felt two cold draughts of air, and she sneezed loudly twice in a row. This awoke her husband.

As soon as he woke up, he told his wife, "I know now who those two half people are." They had shown themselves very clearly to him. They had also started to attack him, one on each side. That was why he was violently struggling to fight them off.

It turned out that in his younger years he was a sailor. During one of his voyages, he gambled and won a lot of money from two fellow workers. Those two people lost everything to him, including all of their wages and savings.

When the gambling was over, he started back to his cabin to go to bed, but the two people had been waiting outside in ambush. After he had walked outside only a short distance, the two sprang on him and started beating him. Perhaps they were mad at losing the money, or perhaps they wanted to rob him. In any case, they started beating him violently.

He had no choice but to resist --- this was his explanation. As he was fiercely fighting off the two men, the two attackers fell, slipping to the side of the ship. It so happened that just then a huge wave came up and the bow of the ship tipped, sliding the two men into the water. Unfortunately, the angle at which they slid into water landed them right next to the rotors. Trapped by the turning rotors, their upper bodies were smashed to pieces.

After witnessing the two workers' upper bodies being mashed up, the man became very frightened and ran back to his room without alerting anyone. For many years, he carried this secret in his heart. But, as more than twenty years passed, this incident also faded from his memory.

Two years ago, these two spirits finally tracked him down and followed him home. They wanted him to pay back their lives. That was why, in his dream, he kept saying that he would give them his life. But they replied, "You only have one life, we want two lives!" He asked them, "What am I going to do? I only have one life." Not too long after that dream, his daughter broke an arm, and many other problems also descended upon their family. Not knowing why they were having such bad luck, they decided to come to me for help.

Water Ghosts for Eighteen Years

The two ghastly spirits, both young men, were standing next to him. They showed their bloodied and mangled bodies to me. One of them spoke, "You cannot interfere with this! He owes us his life, and he must pay back!" They said that I absolutely must not intervene on his behalf.

I kept reasoning with them, "Since you have come here, a place for resolving karmic hatred, do not continue to engage in actions that will keep the vicious cycle going. Now you seek revenge, next he will seek revenge, when will it ever end?" I tried to mediate for them. One of them replied, "Do you know how horrible it has been for us? After the mutilation of our bodies, we were trapped for eighteen years in the ocean as water ghosts and had to be bullied by water creatures and other souls who have died in the water." I could feel their intense suffering.

After eighteen years, when the run of their fate as water ghosts was over, they went all out to avenge their deaths, searching for the man responsible. Their desire for revenge was very strong. It took them five years to find him. After eighteen years as water ghosts and five years searching, they finally located him twenty-three years after the incident. After hearing my proposition to resolve the karmic enmity between them, one of the ghosts said, "All right, he must offer to do Bardo services for me one thousand times before this debt can be resolved!"

Let me ask all of you, for how many Bardo services have you signed up your own karmic enemies and ancestors? If you killed someone in a past life, then how long would it take you to do all these Bardo services? I did some computation and realized that would be impossible! One could tell that the couple did not have a strong foundation in spiritual practice, and their roots in Buddhism were very shallow. They just walked into the door, and it would take some time before they would be able to face their own karma! I thought to myself, "That is impossible! It will be lucky if they come to participate in even one or two Bardo services. A thousand times is just impossible!"

I offered, "That is impossible! How about this ..." The other flatly refused, "You absolutely must not get involved! We know you can help him, but we are going to make him pay us back!" They were very fierce and tough.

I asked the husband, "When did this happen?" He thought and said, "I have been in the United States for twenty-three years, and the incident had happened about three to four years before I came to the States. It was twenty-six years ago." He wished for a resolution, and I asked him to try the divination blocks. After trying many times, the answers were negative because they had not yet taken refuge. It is very difficult for someone who has not taken refuge to put his heart and mind into doing the homework and meritorious deeds that I recommend. His two attached spirits also knew that it would be impossible for him to do these deeds.

I could only suggest to the couple that they first take refuge. And not just the husband and wife, but they would also have to sign up the two attached karmic enemies, the three "aborted" spirits in the underworld, as well as their three living children. This was to ensure that the seeds of Buddhism will be sowed in their consciousness. Then I proceeded to give him the homework. But I was thinking to myself, "As they have never been in touch with this teaching before, this list of homework assignments is only a piece of paper to them. Will they be able to carry it out?"

Persuading the Attached Spirits

I was hoping the two attached spirits would promptly let go of their hatred, so I turned to them, "If this person does not start doing spiritual practice to purify his karma, he will eventually meet his own retribution. You don't have to harm him now to get even. Come and do the spiritual practice on your own. If you are able to let him go, this kind of forgiveness and caring for another person is a meritorious act. A magnanimous heart that refrains from inflicting further pain on others will bring more blessing, fortune, and light to you and help you be reborn to a better realm. You also will not fall further down and continue any more entanglement with him."

The hatred of one of the attached spirits' was particularly strong, and I could not make him budge at all. I prayed to the Buddhas and Bodhisattvas to bless them so they would be able to come for the Bardo deliverance services. I told the husband, "There will be a Bardo service here at the temple next week." [Master Samantha took a look at the congregation present.] But I don't see him here now. How can we help him? He is unable to make it even the first time!

The couple left, and I don't know what has happened to them. Now I am in a tug-of-war to pull the two attached spirits over. I tell them, "Let go, don't fight with them, and you will get the eternal Light. Since they don't do any spiritual practice, their own karmic retribution will eventually catch up with them."

Appendix

Dharma (Volume 1)

Impressions of
Master Samantha

Written by Vincent Eng Koh, a student from Malaysia,
and originally published in Chinese
in the Special Issue of the 10th Annual
Celebration of Purple Lotus Temple in 1997.

Translated by Janny Chow.

It was 1991 when Master Samantha first came to Malaysia to teach the Dharma. The wonderful teachings and miraculous events surrounding her visit at that time won many people over. Afterwards, the students there hoped very much to invite Master to visit Malaysia again.

Therefore, in 1994, entrusted by the Dharma-chakra Society of Kuala Lumpur, I made a trip to San Francisco to invite Master to return to Malaysia for another teaching. Prior to that trip, although I had heard a great deal about Master Samantha and the famous Purple Lotus Temple, I had not had any opportunity to get to know Master well. My interactions with her had been limited to general greetings (with my palms joined respectfully in the Buddhist way) when I ran into her many times during the biannual ceremonies held in Redmond, Washington.

After hearing the intent of my visit, Master agreed right away to visit Malaysia again. Because of this trip, I was also able to have a long talk with Master. My first impression was that she was an affable, frank, forthright, verbose, and powerful lady, not unlike some of the superwomen of the modern era, but completely without arrogance. She is a genuine master who not only talks the talk, but also walks the walk. Her speech and actions reflect her sincerity, generosity, and compassion, as well as a noble fearlessness in situations of crises. Later on, I was able to accompany and observe Master on many dharma trips and gained a deeper understanding about her.

I still have a vivid memory of the unusual events that occurred during Master's second trip to Malaysia, and I would like to share some of these here.

First of all, on March 21, 1994, soon after Master's arrival at Kuala Lumpur, rain started falling heavily for two days, bringing a cool relief to the long drought and high temperatures (35 degree Celsius) that had been plaguing the area. The rain continued for five days. Later on, at the farewell dinner, when a government official attending the party told Master that the city was prone to floods, Master immediately stood up to apologize in front of the thousand attendees. She publicly announced her wish that the Dragon Kings would lighten up the rain the next day. Indeed, the following day, the rain turned into a drizzle and it continued that way until April 1st, the day Master departed, and the blazing hot sun returned again.

In another incident, when Master arrived at the Tian Xian Society located at the city of Bukit Mertajam, near Penang, the leader of the local chapter asked Master as soon as he greeted her when she would come again. Master answered casually, "It all depends on the Heavens. If the people here have an affinity with me, then there will be rain." Master had spoken those words inside the main hall at the local Kek Lok Si Temple. At that time, the sky above was bright and sunny, without a trace of cloud. Fifteen minutes later, dark clouds suddenly appeared above our heads, shrouding the temple. This was followed by a showering of rain!

Another similar event happened at the Wanfa Society at the city of Miri in East Malaysia. During the Dragon King Vase Offering ceremony, aureoles of rainbow light appeared in the bright, cloudless sunny sky. This was followed by the appearance of rainbows three times a day for the next several days. When Master gave a public teaching at the Ipoh Hotel, many pictures taken of her when developed showed light emanating from her. Even the local newspapers New Life Post and Life Media published the light photographs and headlined them with bold captions.

Finally, I would like to cite another interesting event that I witnessed. In May 1995, when Master revisited Malaysia, a group of more than ten students, me included, took Master to visit Lake Kenyir at Kuala Terengganu. At that time, the fish farm was packed full with several hundreds of "Toman" (snakehead) fishes, each about two feet long. Tossing and turning in the water, the fishes were causing a din by hitting their bodies against the water. Master Samantha then asked us to perform the Fourfold Refuge Taking and Great Ocean Deliverance Visualization and chant mantras for the fishes. She hoped that through the empowerment of the mantras, the fishes would be able to engender an affinity with the Buddhas and encounter a pathway in the future to reach liberation. Just as everyone closed their eyes to visualize and chant the mantras, the thrusting fishes suddenly stopped thrashing and came to a complete standstill. It was an unusual scene—as if they were listening and praying together with us—and an incredible experience for all observing. As soon as everyone finished chanting and released their mudras, the fishes returned to their previous state of thrusting and jumping. Quite miraculous!

There were too many interesting phenomena during Master's dharma trip for me to describe each of them in detail. Perhaps some people would think all these are just coincidences. But, isn't it miraculous that so many coincidences occurred around Master Samantha? In my opinion, this demonstrates the power of the True Buddha Tantric Dharma. As long as one is sincerely reliant on the Root Guru and diligently practices accordingly, one will engender the spiritual power and receive support and protection from the Lineage Guru, Personal Deities, and Dharma Protectors.

Students who have visited Malaysia are aware that the local students there are not very wealthy. Many of them have pitched in to help with the rent and expenses of the local chapters and opened their own homes for others to do group practice. The source of donations is very limited. Often times, the local chapters do not even have the whole collection of Grand Master's books, or any of the audios or videos of his teachings. The chapters are only open on Saturdays for group practice, and they are not open during other times to help students who might come across questions in their practice. There was even one student who had been practicing for ten years and his only wish was to be able to travel to the Ling Shen Ching Tze in Redmond, Washington to meet with Grand Master in person. We all wish very much to have more masters and monks and nuns to come to Malaysia to teach us how to deepen our practice.

Master Samantha is empathetic of our situation. Often times, she declines to accept donations from the local chapters made to her (although the financial situation at the Purple Lotus Temple is also very tight). On the contrary, she even chips in her own money to give back to the chapter. It is her hope that the local students will become independent and stronger, so they can help disseminate the Buddha dharma. Not only that, when Master returns to the United States, she even makes offering out of her own pocket to Grand Master on behalf of the local chapter, so that local chapter will receive Grand Master's blessings!

Many students like to hear Master Samantha's teachings. Apart from gaining a great deal of knowledge into the workings of the spiritual world, what attracts them is that Master's teachings are never boring. Her talks are spontaneous and never scripted and she teaches according to the audience, time, and place. Her understanding of the True Buddha Tantric Dharma has penetrated beyond external liturgies, and she is able to explain the true meaning of the practices precisely and concisely from various angles, using various analogies.

Take the Bardo ceremonies for example. Most students think that they only need to fill out the registration forms then just sit there passively during the ceremony. They are not aware that there are still many "processes" that they can get involved in, working together with the conducting master, Buddhas and Bodhisattvas, and the spirits being delivered, to produce the best outcome from the deliverance services.

Also, most of us have the habit of making offerings using visualization. This is of course acceptable. But, how many of us have tried to make a real bountiful offering which will bring us enhanced and continuous blessing in return? Also, what is the most efficacious way of doing fire offerings to attain the greatest spiritual response? How can one fulfill the wishes in one's heart?

To all the puzzling questions we have in our practices, Master Samantha offers us her unique understanding and interpretation through her teachings. This serves imperceptibly to enhance our wisdom and shorten the time needed for searching. It has also inspired and energized many students in their faith and immersed them into the practice and propagation of the dharma.

Apart from her miraculous powers and popular discourses, many students are in awe of Master's inexhaustible energy during her dharma trips. The organizations that have invited Master to teach at their local chapters have never failed to plan the busiest itinerary, as if they were trying to squeeze every single drop of juice from a piece of sugar cane. In one record trip, Master visited in one month thirty-three local chapters throughout the whole of Malaysia to conduct group practices!

I remember one occasion when Master had to take an early morning flight and then a long bus ride to reach a newly established local chapter. As soon as she arrived, she started giving spiritual consultations until it was time for group cultivation in the evening. Then the next day, she got up at dawn to travel to another local chapter to repeat the same activities again. Not only did she give oral discourses, empowerments, transmit practices on behalf of Grand Master, and counseling, she actually got down to the nitty-gritty business aspects of teaching members how to run their chapter---organizing fund-raisers for them, helping to set up altars, and conducting ceremonies. Even during meal times, she talked to people compassionately to help mediate inter-personal problems among members and give them encouragement. Almost every day and in every stop, she was busy till late at night. When she returned to her hotel, she would still have to answer her mail and do practices and meditate for others and for herself (to cleanse the negative karmic energy she had to take over from providing spiritual consultations and interventions). Many times from my room next to hers, I could hear the sound of vajra bells ringing at 4 or 5 a.m..

In fact, that dharma trip was so arduous that every monk, nun, and student (me included) accompanying Master on the trip was stressed and fatigued. Yet Master was always full of energy and never once complained of being tired. Out of curiosity a student one time asked Master how she was able to keep up with all these tasks with so little sleep and rest. Did Grand Master transmit her any special practice to enable her to have such an inexhaustible source of energy?

Master explained that she was only able to do this due to the blessing and empowerment of the Root Guru, Buddhas and Bodhisattvas, and Dharma Protectors. More importantly, she simply puts 110% into everything she does! Also, her past "near-death experience" has helped her gain a deep understanding of "impermanence." She treasures every person she encounters and wishes to devote the rest of her life to help all beings. In her own words, "Perhaps in this life of mine, I only have this one opportunity to come into contact with the people living here in this area. If I don't seize this moment, it may be hundreds and thousands of eons before we meet again. If one misses the salvation provided by the True Buddha Tantric Dharma in this life, when will one have another opportunity?"

Master is so warm and approachable, open, kind, and energetic that she is deeply loved by the students in Malaysia. In 1995, her trip to Malaysia coincided with Grand Master's birthday. Usually each local chapter celebrates that day in their own way. Master hoped that all students in Malaysia would get together to have a group celebration citing the "power of unity." Although she knew fully well that this was very difficult, she explained, "As long as we really want it, it will happen. The higher beings are all observing us. We are doing this to show them that we can do it. Human life is limited, but the sky is limitless. The sky is infinite and boundless and encompasses everything. We have to learn to become as expansive and tolerant as the sky, and in this way, our accomplishments will live forever!"

Later, in a short two weeks period, through Master's great encouragement and the hard work of many students, more than one thousand students from twenty local chapters in Malaysia took the unprecedented step of coming together to celebrate Grand Master's birthday in a hall with one hundred and twenty-three banquet tables. That time, Master invited all the leaders of the chapters onto the stage to read the True Buddha Sutra and chant the Guru's Heart Mantra together. It was so moving and exhilarating that the memory is still fresh in my mind today. I believe that everyone who had attended the event that time will never forget that one moment when our hearts and hands joined together and the sense of separation between self and others seemed to have vanished!

During the last several years of indefatigable teaching around the world, Master has gained a lot of love and support. But, she has also become the target of slander. Perhaps this is due to her candid style of speech? Master has no fear talking about things that many people have on their minds but do not have the courage to bring up. She is fearless in undertaking tasks that many people wish to do but lack the courage to undertake. Because of this, some people have felt offended. I once asked Master how she managed to face such slander and obstacles along the path. She replied, "I do not look at challenges as challenges. I look at them as learning opportunities and I welcome them with a heart of thankfulness. The sentient beings are actually helping me become an adept. They afford me the opportunity to self reflect and to become more forgiving and tolerant. This is a great chance to learn to yield and surrender oneself to the flow. Therefore, I am only thankful of everything and have no grievance or complaints at all."

Her teaching made me feel embarrassed about my own thoughts. It also enabled me to look at the so-called slandering and rumors with a new perspective. Without the unenlightened sentient beings, I realized, there would be no enlightened Buddha; without the great slandering, there would be no great accomplishment! Other people are only hurting us to help us become enlightened, and we have only ourselves to blame by creating our own demons!

Apart from her speech and conduct, what has also attracted my attention is the Purple Lotus Temple founded by Master. I have always wanted to know how the local chapter is run and how it is able to accomplish so much--including the publishing of the monthly Purple Lotus Journal, the running of a publishing company, an art and craft store, a dormitory, a vegetarian restaurant, and also now the Purple Lotus Buddhist School.

I have in the past learned about the history of the Purple Lotus Temple by reading its monthly journals. It was only two years ago when I first visited the place myself. What I discovered was a fully structured organization with a governing board and committee run with the help of an updated computer system. All income and expenditures are recorded according to rules and regulations. All high cost expenditures need to be approved at committee meetings. Rumors that funding was controlled by private individuals are unfounded. The non-profit status granted to Purple Lotus Temple only came by after all the government requirements and regulations were met.

In the temple, besides the board members and committee members, there are also many monks, nuns, and volunteers. Since there is so much to be done, many of the members multi-task and work very hard. What is rare is that they all are able to maintain a heart of joy and a mind continuously turned towards the Buddha, Dharma, and Virtue.

From interacting with them, I also observe that they have absolute faith, respect, and reliance on the Root Guru. They have great respect for Master Samantha and work with her as a team. I believe this is because Master lives what she teaches, and she also is very fair, forgiving, and kind. This naturally brings out a group effort and desire amongst all involved to bring the task at hand to completion.

I also would like to pay special tribute to Andrew Chou, Master's husband. Andrew has been there for Master from the beginning, accompanying her on this arduous cultivation path. Apart from giving Master financial and spiritual support, he has made a great deal of personal sacrifices. Because Master spends so much time teaching the dharma around the world, Andrew has taken on the difficult dual role of being a father and mother to their children. Master has always emphasized "self sacrifice" and "serving others." Many people have misunderstood her and accused her of neglecting her family. I personally am very appreciative of Andrew for his tolerance and magnanimous gestures in allowing Master to walk on this path to help more sentient beings.

To my best knowledge, the Purple Lotus Buddhist School is founded upon the spirit of the True Buddha Tantric Dharma with the goal of remedying deficiencies in the current educational system. Master Samantha recognizes that current mainstream education places too much emphasis on materialistic achievements and fails to cultivate in the students a moralistic and introspective bearing. Students study to pursue fame and profit and have no knowledge of the workings of karma and transmigration. As a result, we see in the world today utilitarianism, spiritual anemia, and moral degeneration. There is an urgent need to establish a recognized alternate educational model demonstrating the great spiritual accomplishment and humanistic philosophy of our Root Guru. This educational institute will allow people to study, research, and practice the True Buddha Tantric Dharma. With the training of more personnel who are proficient in teaching the dharma, a new paradigm in education will be created and usher in a new and moralistic society.

It has occurred to me that Grand Master had attained a breakthrough in his cultivation after he immigrated to the United States and secluded himself in extended retreat and deep meditation. I am sure Master Samantha realizes the need for such practices. Yet, because of her compassion for others and various other reasons, she has not had an opportunity to do an extended retreat to reach higher spiritual realization. Master, here I would like to make a heartfelt wish that when the time is ripe, you will be able to take a long retreat, and that when you re-emerge, you will be able to arrive at even greater accomplishment!

Offerings from Purple Lotus Temple
A Local Chapter of True Buddha School
in San Francisco Bay Area

Regular Hours of Operation
Daily from 10:00am to 4:00pm

Regular Programs
Group cultivation every Saturday at 8:00pm
Bardo Deliverance ceremonies when announced (call for more information)
Sutra chanting every first and fifteenth of the lunar month, with merits dedicated to those who have registered for Annual Blessing Lights and Planet Guardian's protection

General Services
Registration for the Annual Planet Guardian's protection
Setting up altars to dedicate merits to one's ancestors,
attached spirits, and the spirits of aborted fetuses

Services by Appointment
Personal consultation with Master Samantha Chou
Energized talismans available

Other scheduled activities
Repentance and blessing ceremonies
Fire offering (Homa) ceremonies
Water offering ceremonies

Complimentary publications available at PLT
True Buddha News (Chinese)
Annual Almanac (Chinese)
Free pamphlets on Buddhist teachings
For blessing ceremony and Bardo Deliverance
registration forms, please contact us and we will mail or
fax them to you. The forms are also available on-line at:
www.purplelotus.org

Gift shop on site
Buddhist statues, books, incense, music and mantra CD
available.

Purple Lotus Temple
636 San Mateo Avenue, San Bruno, California 94066, USA.
Tel: (650) 952-9513, Fax: (650) 952-9567
www.purplelotus.org

Purple Lotus Buddhist School is now accepting Applications!

Come join the first Chinese and English Bilingual and Buddhist School in the San Francisco Bay Area, and select for your children an education that will exert a positive influence on them for the rest of their lives.

An independent, coeducational boarding school for grades 1-12 in the Buddhist tradition;
- Academic programs designed to support both college preparatory and spiritual learning students;
- Student to teacher ratio is 6:1;
- Culturally diverse student population;
- Awarded by Union City for special achievement in community services;
- Emphasis on values, character, leadership, ethics and self-esteem at all grade levels;
- Safe, secure and supportive environment;
- Support programs to coach students in developing a harmonious mind, healthy body, and compassionate spirit.

For applications or additional information about the Purple Lotus Buddhist School contact:

Purple Lotus Buddhist School
33615 9th Street, Union City, CA 94587
Tel: (510) 429-8808, Fax: (510) 429-7150